# E. M. Delafield

## Twayne's English Authors Series

Kinley E. Roby, Editor

*Northeastern University*

TEAS 408

E. M. DELAFIELD
(1890–1943)
*Photograph by Stuart Black*

# E. M. Delafield

## By Maurice L. McCullen

*University of the Pacific*

*Twayne Publishers* • *Boston*

*E. M. Delafield*

Maurice L. McCullen

Copyright © 1985 by G. K. Hall & Company
All Rights Reserved
Published by Twayne Publishers
A Division of G. K. Hall & Company
70 Lincoln Street
Boston, Massachusetts 02111

Book Production by Elizabeth Todesco
Book Design by Barbara Anderson

Printed on permanent/durable acid-free
paper and bound in the United States of
America.

**Library of Congress Cataloging in Publication Data**

McCullen, Maurice L.
  E. M. Delafield.

  (Twayne's English authors series; TEAS 408)
  Bibliography: p. 136
  Includes index.
  1. Delafield, E. M., 1890–1943—Criticism and interpretation.
  2. Women in literature.   3. Feminism and literature.
  I. Title.   II. Series.
PR6007.E33Z77   1985      823'.912      85–801
ISBN 0–8057–6899–8

# Contents

*About the Author*
*Preface*
*Chronology*

## About the Author

Maurice McCullen lives in Stockton, California, where he teaches graduate and undergraduate courses in English for the University of the Pacific. After military service, he completed his doctoral work at the University of Colorado and taught at the University of Kentucky. His areas of interest are nineteenth- and twentieth-century English literature, and his scholarly articles have dealt primarily with the English novel.

# Preface

Just before Christmas in 1943, an England at war paused to commemorate the passing of E. M. Delafield, "The Provincial Lady," and then forgot her. Only those who reached adulthood during World War II are likely to remember her now, and they remember her with affection. One Londoner recalls switching on her radio during a dark day in 1941 to find out if the world had actually collapsed. Instead of the usual dose of gloom, she heard Delafield saying, "Hello, this is the kitchen front— and this is the Provincial Lady wrestling with it." "She *was* an inspiration," the Londoner sighed, recalling Delafield's wit, which on that occasion comically concluded that housewives should believe none of the BBC news and something less of what their husbands reported at dinner.

Novelist, playwright, journalist, tireless lecturer, radio commentator—E. M. Delafield spoke to and for women throughout her career. The near extinction of her reputation now seems unfair, especially when friends like Vera Brittain and Winifred Holtby have recently been "rediscovered."

Delafield was an eminent woman of letters who believed that her talents should serve her country and her countrywomen. Throughout her career she addressed feminine issues, particularly of women in their domestic roles, and she achieved a reputation as a spokeswoman for women's concerns. She reflected female points of view so centrally and accurately that, for instance, her "Home is Like That" series for the BBC, which pleased London listeners, was still being rebroadcast years after her death. Her serious fiction also grew in reputation, but she reached an even wider audience in her humorous writing. Through a variety of literary avenues, Delafield was a distinct literary and social "presence" in England, particularly from 1930 until her death.

Her death and a rapidly changing world brought about quick critical oblivion, and her work is almost unknown today. This loss of reputation is partly attributable to the fact that she wrote too much—as she herself admitted publicly—diffusing her talent in too many modes and projects. Her domestic subjects from a feminine perspective were sometimes dispensed with as pap for the ladies. Only since the rise of a feminine critical approach can such fiction secure serious attention. Much of her best humor appeared in weekly magazines and was soon lost to view, as is the case with even the best journalism. Finally, her best work comes directly out of her own experience and requires the aid of biography for satisfactory explication. In discussing Delafield, one cannot avoid the vexed question of the significance of the writer's own experiences in her work. Recent women's criticism, fortunately, has focused attention on the woman behind the work, so that this issue need not be debated here.

Delafield dealt repeatedly with "universal female experience of the kind that does not get into the novels formalist critics value."[1] She has paid a heavy price for her determined adherence to domestic realism, but it is the contention of this study that the price should not include critical oblivion.

This study has, accordingly, a polemical bias. Although many of Delafield's novels cannot stand alone, they are important data in the formation of a life's work that can. And although her wit and humor are scattered about in novels, plays, journalism, talks, and lectures, discussion supported by a sufficient number of examples may demonstrate that she was a first-rate humorist. Her place as a social critic in what is now seen as a "women's literary tradition" needs to be established, and to this end there is needed a primary bibliography and accurate descriptions of each book and a discussion of where they fit in Delafield's oeuvre.

Thus, the thesis that this forgotten woman of letters has not received sufficient critical recognition is prosecuted developmentally. A survey discussion of her first sixteen novels follows the necessary and heretofore generally unknown biographical background. Although most of these early novels are rather slow-moving and old-fashioned, this first attempt at reappraisal mentions them all in the context of her growth and development as a writer.

Her complementary development into "the perfect light" in journalism, which led to a best-seller and a more dramatic, polished novel form is addressed in chapters 4 and 5. The *Diary of a Provincial Lady* is more than a best-seller. A rarity in these days of critical saturation, it is a forgotten classic. Together with their sequels, the "Provincial Lady" books deserve a special place in literary history.

Chapters 6 and 7 deal with Delafield's novels of the thirties, her wartime journalism, and her last novels. This polished work shows her at the height of her power, and its close involvement with its historical period makes it a valuable sociocultural record. *Thank Heaven Fasting* is a definitive portrait of the Edwardian period. An accurate ironic chronicle of the formation by tradition of an upper-class woman, it is another minor classic.

The last chapter presents perspectives on Delafield's achievement, particularly in the area of humor. As most of her work is out of print (there seems to be only one available copy of *The Bazalgettes*), this first reappraisal has of necessity been descriptive as well as critical. Extensive use of quotation is included to give the reader a feeling for her technique and vision, and the range and quality of her humor. I close with a beginning analysis of her humorous technique and argue for the reestablishment of her reputation.

The difficulties in presenting this prolific, delightful, unknown woman of letters for reconsideration have been large ones. I am convinced that her accomplishment is greater than the sum of its parts. But there are so many parts. The Twayne Series is justly famous for its complete coverage of important minor writers, and it will be pleasing to many to see E. M. Delafield take her place among them. I am grateful for Twayne's understanding, particularly that of Emily McKeigue and Dr. Kinley Roby.

Additional debts for help in preparing this study are many. First to my long-suffering family. Next, I received kind, patient assistance from a number of people who guided me through uncharted territory. Diana Parikian unselfishly shared with me all of the materials she had collected for her own study of Delafield. Hamish Hamilton more than once took time to answer my many questions. Marjorie Watts, a delightful resource person, helped me to place Delafield in London literary and social circles, and the Kentisbeare villagers helped me to see her as she was at home. Most of the necessary background for a study of this most autobiographical writer came from Rosamund Dashwood, Delafield's daughter, who generously gave privileged information in spite of the fact that, like the rest of her family, she does not want her mother's life written about.

For other research assistance, my warmest thanks to Anne Yandle and Joan Selby at the library of the University of British Columbia; Challice Reed, assistant program information director at the BBC London; Sheila McIlwraith and A. D. Peters & Co. Ltd.; Mr. Richard Price and *Punch* magazine; and Terence Pepper of the National Portrait Gallery. My special thanks to Laura Boyer and Judy Andrews of the University of the Pacific for their immense helpfulness, and to the university for its support through faculty research grants.

Maurice L. McCullen

*University of the Pacific*

# Chronology

1890    Edmeé Elizabeth Monica de la Pasture born to Mr. and Mrs. Henry de la Pasture (Comte Henri du Carel de la Pasture) at Hove, near Brighton, on 9 June.

ca. 1908–1910    Debut in London; debutante years.

ca. 1911–1913    Convent life in Belgium.

1914    Member of the Volunteer Aid Detachment in Exeter. Begins her first novel during lunch breaks in the garden of the Rougemont Hotel.

1917    *Zella Sees Herself* published by Heineman, the first publisher to read it. Serves with the Ministry of National Service at Bristol.

1919    Marries Arthur Paul Dashwood, son of Sir George Dashwood, sixth baronet. Goes to Singapore with husband.

1920    Son Lionel born.

1921    Returns to England; settles in Devonshire.

1922    May, begins as book reviewer for *Time and Tide.*

1923    Publishes first article in *Time and Tide.* Dashwoods rent Croyle, their home near Kentisbeare in Devon, in September and purchase it in July.

1924    Daughter Rosamund born. First short story for *Time and Tide.*

1925    Appointed justice of the peace for Devonshire.

1927    Becomes a director of *Time and Tide.*

1929    "The Provincial Lady" makes her appearance in *Time and Tide* on 6 December.

1930    *The Diary of a Provincial Lady,* Delafield's
        nineteenth published book, a best-seller in
        England and America. Her first play, *To See
        Ourselves,* has long run at the Ambassador's
        Theater.

1932    Begins to write for *Punch.*

1933    Lectures in the United States. Serializes "The
        Provincial Lady in America."

1936    Visits Russia.

1937    Second American lecture tour.

1940    Death of son Lionel on active service. Ap-
        pointed speaker for the Ministry of Informa-
        tion.

1943    Dies at Croyle of cancer on 11 December.

## Chapter One

# The Life:
# Materials for Fiction

Edmeé Elizabeth Monica de la Pasture—who later wrote under the pseudonym E. M. Delafield—was born in 1890 into upper-class British society, the eldest daughter of Count Henri Philip du Carel de la Pasture, whose family settled in England after the French Revolution. Her mother, Elizabeth Lydia Rosabelle Bonham, who was descended from Kentish squires, married the count in 1887 at the age of twenty-one after her first, and highly successful, debutante season.

Count Henri, as an émigré nobleman, was shut off in England from the normal careers suitable for a titled gentleman; he was never seen to work at anything. His title could not even be officially recognized, and his lovely and ancient name became anglicized to Henry Delapature. He was a handsome, charming, and talented man, and his daughter adored him. His wife remained a social belle throughout most of her life, her wit and charm praised by celebrities from William S. Gilbert to Noel Coward. She began to write soon after her marriage and became almost as popular as she was prolific, often publishing several novels and plays in the same year. During Edwardian days she sparkled socially on both sides of the Atlantic, and her granddaughter, Rosamund Dashwood, remembers her in the thirties as "a petite, jolie-laide," very lively, witty, and irreverent.[1]

## Family Conflict

Mrs. de la Pasture's daughters remembered her differently. Although she was no ogre, neither was she a good mother. Her sharp wit, possessiveness, and tendency to dominate made it impossible for her daughters (Irlande ["Yoe"] followed Edmeé by one year) to develop naturally. She had wanted boys, and expressed dissatisfaction with her shy, gawky girls often and publicly. Their situation did not help: a disengaged father, a furiously engaged mother; they were "half foreign" and Catholic to boot. They never really felt that they belonged, either at home or outside it; and they early developed an emotional dependence on one another that caused them to turn inward even more. Theirs was a touching, extremely close relationship that was ultimately unhealthy for their development.

The de la Pasture household was strict and old-fashioned even for that day. Every Victorian prohibition seems to have been a part of their upbringing: stern rules, awkward and old-fashioned clothing, strict observance of religious dogma. The de la Pasture daughters were never free from the familial and societal dictates designed to train upper-class girls to take their place in good society. One governess, to check Edmeé's habit of "drooping," set up a nailed board behind her desk chair. As long as she sat erect, she could not feel the nails, but if she slouched they dug into her back. Edmeé was allowed little freedom at home and none at the convent schools to which she was sent at age ten, first in England and then in Belgium.

Edmeé was withdrawn from school in 1907 to make her debut and to enter the same tense, competitive marriage market that Dickens and Thackeray had deplored fifty years earlier. She was not a success. Her only proposal came from a boy her mother decided "didn't mean anything" (i.e., lacked the requisite social position).

During her second season, Yoe made her debut and her beloved father died, making a bad experience utterly traumatic. Her mother's irritation with her daughters was openly discussed in their social circles. Outwardly shy and awkward, emotionally dependent upon one another, neither girl was a success in the only occupation open to women of their class: obtaining a husband. The added weight of grief and mourning undid them completely. Edmeé drifted into a sort of social limbo, making the social round as an awkward appendage of her widowed mother. She had no sense of self, no purpose in life, and nothing to look forward to.

All of this is clearly deducible from the early novels and from her classic novel of Edwardian society, *Thank Heaven Fasting.* She wrote so close to her life in these books that her unhappy childhood became common knowledge, the one biographical fact that this private woman freely acknowledged. It is nearly the only source of knowledge about her life, a fact known even to casual friends like Dame Rebecca West.

But Edmeé's unhappiness continued. Less than two years later her mother married Sir Hugh Clifford, colonial secretary of Ceylon. Her daughters learned of the marriage only after its consummation, and Lady Clifford then left for Ceylon after the briefest of good-byes. There was no place for two gawky young women in the life of the first lady of the colony, and the girls were packed off to the country house of Lady Clifford's younger sister, "dear Aunt Connie, in Cornwall."

Subsequent developments might have ended Edmeé's story. She turned to religion, seemingly the only alternative to a purposeless existence. She was lonely, hurt, and confused, trapped by family and class, and a social failure in her own eyes. She looked to religion as a vocation. She had been devout as a schoolgirl; and now, on reaching twenty-one, joined a French religious order.

## The Bride of Heaven

Edmeé concealed this period of her life, as Dickens did his days at Warren's Blacking Warehouse; however, a fairly accurate record of this period can be pieced together from early novels and a play, *The Glass Wall.* In addition, a surprising document in the Delafield Collection at the University of British Columbia clarifies matters still further. It is the anonymous record—in the form of a twenty-eight-page typescript entitled "Brides of Heaven"—of the convent years of an unnamed narrator, and appears from internal evidence to have been written in the early thirties, probably for Edmeé's friend, Lorna Lewis, who returned it to the family after E. M. Delafield's death.[2]

"Brides of Heaven" sets forth the reasons for choosing to become a nun, and details conventual life in a flat, unadorned style. It is a compelling document and moving record of young Edmeé's convent years. For example, a rule enjoined silence upon the community except for forty minutes at midday and thirty minutes at night. It prescribed certain mortifications of the flesh as punishment for breaking any rules of the order. These included flagellation, kneeling with the arms held straight

out from the sides, and "the bracelet," a barbed circlet worn
about the elbow: "The pressure, after a little while, became
agonizing." Convent conditions were harsh and unsanitary; but
for the first time Edmeé's life acquired a sense of purpose and
became endurable, sometimes enjoyable.

Less endurable were the efforts to obliterate the self. The
nuns viewed any illness or weakness as sinful and reprimanded
the novices for signs of friendship. Common formulae like "il
me semble" or "je pense" received instant rebuke. Nor could
a novice refer to "ma dejeuner"; it was "notre dejeuner."

The novice-mistress strictly censored both outgoing and in-
coming mail. Any endearment or personal confidence was ruth-
lessly expunged, and it was this censorship that led to Edmeé's
renunciation of conventual life. Yoe wrote of her own plan
to become a nun, and the young novice posted a letter of remon-
strance, the last letter allowed until the end of Lent. She found
it in shreds on her bed and was forbidden to rewrite it. Her
brooding over this incident convinced her that she must not
have a true vocation, and she at last made a confession of her
disbelief to the novice-mistress.[3]

Renunciation of her novitiate proved difficult. For some days
her superiors questioned her sincerity, then made her continue
her duty for weeks while they tested her decision. Next, they
gave her over to a Jesuit who at first persuaded gently, then
threatened her with eternal damnation. At last she was allowed
to leave—for another convent, in Rome, at which to reflect
and meditate.

When she left the mother-house, the novice mistress and her
assistant

both said goodbye to me kindly and affectionately, and promised me
their prayers. They felt sure, they said, that one day I should come
back.

I never did. That was twenty years ago. I dream still, from time
to time, of being a postulant in the Noviciate in Belgium, and finding
myself unable to come away.

The ordeal ended. It may have lasted for as long as two years.
During those last agonizing months she lost forty pounds "and
came away looking like a living skeleton."

Edmeé now found only more unhappiness and suffering. Shyer, more nervous, frightened by traffic, bewildered by the rush of daily life—she was unable to cope with the world: "It was the helpless insecurity of one utterly at variance with her surrounding."⁴ She had immediately picked up again all of her old problems, plus a crushing new sense of failure. This part of the story was powerfully re-created half-a-dozen years later in *Consequences*. The ex-nun in this novel, whose despairing reflection is quoted above, ends a suicide. The obvious sincerity of her deathwish stands as a poignant testimony to Edmeé de la Pasture's condition of mind in late 1913. (These experiences haunted her into middle life; old religious ghosts were still being exorcised in *Turn Back the Leaves* [1930] and *The Glass Wall* [1933].)

## World War I: Recovery

Edmeé was saved, ironically, by World War I. She had from childhood disliked the thought of war, and the Great War inspired in her a lifelong feeling of fear and loathing for this barbaric, inhumane activity. But the war gave this lost, sheltered, and immature twenty-four-year-old woman her first worldly experience, and her life changed dramatically. Edmeé may have joined the Volunteer Aid Detachment just before war broke out. In any event, 1914 found her in Exeter on duty as a member of the V.A.D.

The V.A.D. and other women's military auxiliary organizations have recently received much attention. The BBC series *Women at War*, during Queen Elizabeth II's jubilee, was a great success, and scholarly work like Arthur Marwick's study of the same title has demonstrated the contribution to the war effort by Britain's women. The war was a revelation to women of Edmeé's class, for upper-class women had been kept on very short leashes by their families, and now many restraints were suddenly put aside. "Elizabeth," as her friends now called her (only her mother and her aunts continued Edmeé), lived with women and served men she would not formerly have been allowed to speak to. She scrubbed floors, cut sandwiches, and served tea, where before she could only wait for a servant to perform these, and even slighter tasks. Once she took night duty at a great house, now a convalescent hospital, where in her debutante years she had attended a large dancing party. Best of all, these "Very Artful Darlings," as the Tommies called them, were extremely popular; and Elizabeth, thus far a loser in life, had her first sense of belonging to a winning team. Newfound freedom and purpose stimulated her creativity and she began a novel. When other V.A.D.'s went to lunch, Elizabeth went either to the public library or to a park behind the old Rougemont Hotel and wrote. *Zella Sees Herself,* by E. M. Delafield (her pseudonym), was accepted by the first publisher to see the manuscript and appeared in 1917.

Favorable reviews, her own money, a new identity, rebirth— Elizabeth was ecstatic. She often recalled picking up a package of six complimentary copies of her novel at the Exeter Post Office and bicycling furiously around town hoping to find friends to present them to. The surname of her nom de plume is an obvious anglicization of de la Pasture; E. M. an abbreviation of her own initials, though she always said that she chose these initials as a compliment to E. M. Forster, whose work she greatly admired. Her second novel, based on her experiences as a V.A.D., was a greater success a year later.

## Marriage at Last

After the Peace in 1918, she married Major Arthur Paul Dashwood, third son of the sixth baronet. Her friend, Marjorie Watts, remembers that Paul wrote her an appreciative letter praising her novels from his station in the Middle East and sought her out when he returned to England.[5] They were married soon after and sailed for Hong Kong three months later.

Their marriage stands as a tribute to both. Elizabeth was complex, sensitive, and continental in taste. Above all she was an impractical romantic who lived richly in her imagination. Paul Dashwood, in contrast, was a practical, realistic engineer who was willing to leave literature and the arts "to women and other neurotics." Mrs. Watts remembers Elizabeth's premarital worries and the sick terror with which she suffered through her marriage day. Why did this twenty-eight-year-old writer marry at all?

First, Paul loved her and asked her. After what she had suffered, her gratitude must have been immense. And he was obviously a fine man who would care for her. For despite her recent successes, Elizabeth was still a social failure. Only marriage could change the fact that she had failed as a debutante and was fast becoming an old maid. Marriage provided instant social security and guaranteed a freedom denied the single woman. Moreover, she deeply desired the permanency of a home, a husband, and children.

## The Federated Malay States

Paul Dashwood performed his duties as chief engineer for the Hong Kong harbor project superlatively. Afterward, he supervised building the docks at Singapore and again distinguished himself, so that he was placed on the civil lists and awarded the Order of the British Empire.

But these years were not particularly happy ones for Elizabeth. She lived in British compounds sealed off from the rich life around her. Social life centered on the Club, with its gossip, parties, occasional scandal—and once again she did not fit in. She could not even write about it. All of the novels she wrote out East have English settings and draw on her unhappy life before the war. It is an outstanding measure of her rejection of smug colonial life that such rich subject matter was never tapped by this quick and observant writer who usually wrote about events close to her own experience. She did, infrequently, use an Eastern setting for a short story, but in only one of these, a Kiplingesque piece, was the material deeply felt. Occasionally, much later, a bitter or painful remark stemming from this period is given a fictional character; and these strike such a discordant note that they may have been largely unconscious. For example, in a satiric *Punch* sketch, "When Old Friends Meet," the irony points directly at Elizabeth: "Remember that woman in Singapore who'd written a book?" "By Jove, yes! Plainest woman I ever saw in my life. Couldn't ride for toffee."[6]

In 1920, Lionel Paul was born. Elizabeth had her son—but she could not raise him. She would have to deliver him up to an amah, and as early as age eight would be expected to send him to school in England. As she was determined to raise her child herself, after her own unhappy childhood, and to insure that he was secure and loved, a crisis necessarily occurred. Elizabeth was desperate to return home; Paul's career opportunities lay in the East. She may have threatened to leave. In the end, her unhappiness moved Paul to agree to a return. It seems certain that she undertook to ensure their livelihood by writing, at least until he could resume his career. This obligation to Paul, whether expressed or not, joined with a real financial necessity and drove her to ever greater production almost from the moment the family arrived back in England.

## Return to England: Journalism

The Dashwoods soon moved back to Devonshire, and in September 1923 established themselves at Croyle, their new home. A country house of twenty-odd rooms, it stands handsomely on a hill overlooking the little village of Kentisbeare a mile or two away. The family loved the place; and although they had taken it on a yearly tenancy, they bought it before the lease was up. Croyle remained the family home until Elizabeth's death in 1943.

Meanwhile, Paul could not find an engineering position. He became instead an estate agent, overseeing the large Bradfield property bordering Croyle. The end of his professional life, with all of its challenges and accomplishments, and the acceptance of a lesser position, must have hurt him, but he seems not to have complained. Elizabeth, however, recognized the pain she had caused and lacerated herself for it in her later fiction. To pay the bills, she wrote furiously, publishing three novels in two years and a large amount of free-lance journalism. In 1922 she joined Lady Margaret Rhondda's circle of fine writers at *Time and Tide* magazine.

## The Writer

Her writing habits recall those of Anthony Trollope—she wrote constantly. Marjorie Watts remembers her writing a complete short story in a bungalow in Cornwall while the Watts children noisily played ball off the wall behind her. Percy Lane, gardener at Croyle, whose own writing she coached, remembers that she wrote every day she was at home. He still recalls her cheerful industry and the startling fact that he always felt free to interrupt her. Sometimes, indeed, she interrupted herself and talked with him through an open window. Her daughter, Rosamund, also recalls that she wrote all of the time; and her images of E. M. Delafield, seated, pencil in hand, manuscript on lap, can instantly be placed in nearly any room in the house. Again, she not only tolerated but welcomed her children's interruptions—"She was utterly marvellous about that." Rosamund never recalls feeling that she should not interrupt her mother or being chided for doing so.

Rosamund further recalls that her mother was "a perfectionist"—as a career writer rather than as a housewife, for Elizabeth was an impractical housekeeper. Trained only to be a lady, she could not cook, sew, or perform the simplest homemaker's accomplishments. (She did insist upon making "horribly bad coffee" every morning, Rosamund remembers—her one feint at homemaking.) Confronted by any mechanical apparatus (or any arithmetical problem) she "fussed."

Her great friend, novelist Kate O'Brien, stressed the fact that Elizabeth was a "disciplined" perfectionist who answered all letters by hand on the day she received them, scrupulously kept all appointments (and she had many, not only in London, but all over southern England), and "was always up to schedule with her work":

> By some secret power of speed and concentration . . . she'd have answered all that morning's letters before you started, solved all possible domestic hitches, and written an article, or half a chapter. You wouldn't hear about all that—only, you'd get to know that it was so, by getting to know her. And these extra twists that she could put on her own discipline never seemed to affect her sense of fun, or her sheer high spirits.[7]

This picture of Elizabeth completing so much as a letter while the life of the household swirled around her—children, servants, tradespeople, visitors, telephone calls—is awe-inspiring, especially if one envisions a typical period in which she had a play and a novel in hand, deadlines to meet for more than one magazine, a lecture or radio broadcast to prepare, and a healthy amount of correspondence to get through. She wrote too much, as she admitted several times in print. But as we know, she wrote to live. Her pinched circumstances, humorously expressed, are regularly reflected in her journalism until the late thirties.

## Reputation and Fame: A Double Life

Throughout the twenties, Elizabeth supported her family by publishing a novel each year and steadily increasing her output of magazine articles. In 1929, *The Diary of a Provincial Lady* appeared serially in *Time and Tide,* and, as a best-seller in 1930, made her internationally famous. She was by this date a director of *Time and Tide* and had an expanding circle of literary friends in London centered upon the staff and contributors to the magazine. Lady Margaret Rhondda, Winifred Holtby, L. A. G. Strong, A. B. Cox, Mary Agnes Hamilton, Cecily McCall, and others recognized both her charm and her talent, and stimulated in many ways her growth as a person as well as a writer.

As Elizabeth's fame grew, she began to live a kind of double life. Business called her frequently to London, and she became part of its literary ambience—attending literary parties and meetings, giving talks, dining with publishers, holidaying with Lady Rhondda and friends from *Time and Tide.* With all this Paul had nothing to do. Her flat at 57 Doughty Street, across from Dickens's famous home, symbolizes her emancipation, and from 1930 until ill health brought her back to Croyle, she spent much of each year in town.

Although her double life testifies to some disaffection with marriage and family (when interviewed, she was asked invariably what she wanted to be or have been, and she answered just as invariably: "a childless widow"), her London life did not compromise her country life. While her children were away at school she lived in London; she was at home when they were, and numerous pictures of her at games, picnics, and other family outings support remembrances that she always performed her family duties.

Her noblesse oblige sense of duty in the country included the village of Kentisbeare, where she is remembered with genuine affection by everyone who knew her. Although it could hardly be true, considering her usual schedule, several villagers remember that she made Kentisbeare her "number one priority" and that she "adopted the whole life of the community" without reservation. Active in the church, a driving force behind the local Women's Institute, indefatigable caller on shut-ins, Elizabeth made her mark on her village. Time and again, villagers tried to describe to me what it was in "her manner," "her attitude toward people" that inspired an affection that endures. Richard and Anne Milton, who worked for her, still tend the family graves, and, as Mrs. Milton noted, "We often have help."[8]

Paradoxically, although she was as happy at Croyle as she was capable of being ("Devon was where she belonged," her daughter believes), she fitted better in her London circle. A dedicated countrywoman, she did not quite belong there in the sense that she did not fit the pattern for countrywomen of her class. She did not garden, disliked afternoon tea parties, was not politically conservative, loathed horses, and considered hunting to be barbaric. On one occasion, when a fox took refuge in her garden, she refused to allow the hunt into the grounds, saying, "the fox has taken sanctuary." The story would have died it seems had not an indignant neighboring hunting squire kept it going.

Elizabeth's country life extended beyond Kentisbeare of course. She was, for example, justice of the peace for Devon and worked on more than one juvenile crime commission. But her devotion to her private country life and her accomplishments there are all the more remarkable when the other side of her double life is considered. During the seven years before World War II, she was constantly on the move. Two strenuous lecture tours in the United States and a taxing visit to Russia were sandwiched into an increasingly demanding public life in England. Letters to Marjorie Watts reveal a grueling schedule in what seems to have been a fairly typical week in her life: one day in London, meeting with her publishers and literary agent, the next day at home, the following day in Bristol for a BBC radio talk and a Women's Institute lecture, home again for the weekend but concerned about catching the early train to London to complete business at *Time and Tide* so that obligations in Kentisbeare could be satisfied in the late afternoon.

## Portrait

As E. M. Delafield, she was widely known by the early 1930s, and the many descriptions of her mature person and character

allow for a valid composite picture. She was tall, and slender—
five feet seven, with large beautiful hazel eyes (often described
as sad), a trim figure, and fine, delicate, expressive hands. Many
thought her beautiful even in her forties and recalled the tender,
romantic loveliness of her younger years.

A large part of her appeal lay in her manner. Those who
knew her repeatedly described her as "elegant," "perfectly
bred," "like royalty." Summing up this quality, Marjorie Watts
observed: "Ah, you see, you couldn't help that. She just was."
Rosamund would capture this attitude in Elizabeth's definition
of a gentleman: a person "never unintentionally rude." "Elegant
is always a word I would use of her," Rosamund agreed, but
stipulated as well for one of Elizabeth's favorite words—"civilized"—which stood for a whole unwritten attitude toward her
fellow human beings, that attitude Kentisbeare villagers tried
so hard to explain.

While she was charming, vivacious, and very witty—she was
also shy. Hamish Hamilton, the publisher, recalls that even after
she was famous she was afraid to ask her literary agent how
well a particular book was doing. It is not difficult to understand
why people thought her awkward, especially during her confused, immature years. But from earliest childhood the beauty
was there, too. These antithetical perceptions of her persisted
late into her life; and throughout her life the retiring Provincial
Lady coexisted with the London celebrity. Mr. Hamilton, her
close friend, concisely caught the complexity of this lovely
woman: she was, he said, "elegant, attractive, witty, and tragic."
J. B. Priestley, who also described her as lovely and witty, felt
her vulnerability as well, noting that he never knew a woman
"who so obviously needed love."[9] Like other great comic writers, great sadness lay just beneath her wit and irony.

There was one other adjective used to describe Elizabeth
by nearly everyone who knew her—"Courageous."

E. M. Delafield's career during the thirties led from one success to another. She became one of England's best-known humorists, and her reputation grew as a serious novelist. Then
World War II erupted.

Elizabeth was patriotic, often charmingly so. She stood to
attention while the BBC played "God Save the King" after
the nine o'clock news—*and* the national anthems of all the Allies.

As soon as war broke out, she threw herself into her country's service, first as a canteen worker and then as a propagandist for the Ministry of Information. Within a month, the Provincial Lady was welcomed back to the pages of *Time and Tide,* "where she began ten years ago," and where her good-humored criticism of official snafu's helped to smooth over roughnesses in Britian's crash mobilization effort.

She made her major contribution, however, through her weekly *Punch* articles, wringing humor even out of the Blitz and the fear of invasion. The bombings she knew firsthand, for she stuck close to London during the early years of the war, camping out in the Strand over the offices of her literary agent. As she told a Scots newspaperman in 1942, "My wartime job seems to be to go on trying to be funny at all cost."[10]

The cost was heavy, for in November 1940, Lionel died while training with the Devonshire regiment. The Dashwoods never recovered from his death. Nevertheless, the patriotic humorist continued to do her duty. She missed only one week in *Punch* through November and December; and although her Christmas in 1940 was marked by intense mourning, one cannot guess at the depth of her personal tragedy—or of the tragedy itself— from her comic sketches. The courageous wartime service of E. M. Delafield has to this day not been fully recognized.

## Family Life

As so much of E. M. Delafield's fiction came directly from her own experience, and as the center of that experience was family, some understanding of the Dashwoods' life together is necessary to appreciate fully both her writing and her mettlesome spirit. The Dashwoods' marriage does credit to the civilized strength of character of both Elizabeth and Paul. The sensitive, romantic, impractical writer and the stolid, practical, conservative country gentleman worked hard to make their marriage a success. And in a way it was.

Elizabeth's fears about marrying and living with Paul seemed groundless out in the Malay States. She was unhappy there, but not with him. Back in England in 1923, her gratitude for his agreeing to return was great, and despite problems they got on well together. Their changing relationship is faithfully reflected in her work, however, and by the end of the decade, husbands in Delafield fiction partake largely of the officiousness, conventionality, and stultification that elicited so much of her ironic criticism. With the *Diary of A Provincial Lady,* the character was definitively drawn—Robert, the insensitive, avuncular, ultraconservative housemate whose typical response to married life is to fall asleep behind the *Times.* So much acid was used in etching the Robert character (and Paul posed for Arthur Watts's illustrations!) that the Dashwood family was upset. How hurt he himself must have been. Elizabeth gave him the first presentation copy of each of her books, and in his copy of the *Diary* he wrote: "Paul Dashwood / 12.2.30 / (Robert)." Just that. But what iron would enter the soul in acknowledging oneself the original of a consistently satirized character?

Other of his wife's acidic portraits of the husband figure may not have come to his attention. He did not read all of her journalism. But he did accompany her to the Ambassador's Theater to see a production of her first play, *To See Ourselves.* This domestic satire was written at home, and the setting of the play would appear to be Croyle. In the play, the phlegmatic husband at last realized his failures in husbanding and offers belatedly a hint of romance. Paul, the correct gentleman of his day, evidently did not.

There is nothing untoward in the story of their marriage. It is the story of most marriages, perhaps. But Elizabeth yearned all of her life for romantic love—and Paul was not romantic.

Career pressures conspired to further separate the Dashwoods. Throughout the thirties, Elizabeth was often away from home. She had a circle of friends with which her husband had little to do, and he did not accompany her on her trips out of the country. He does not seem to have wanted to. She was more than once urged during these years to locate permanently in London, but for many reasons this course of action was impossible for her. Nevertheless, there was a real estrangement. As her love for her husband cooled, she transferred that love to her son. Lionel Paul (recalling D. H. Lawrence's famous Paul) became the most important man in her life. "A world without Lionel," she wrote to a friend, "is not a world I want to live in."[11] Their relationship was too intense for Lionel to survive.

His story can be found in the novels, particularly *Nothing Is*

*Safe.* A misfit from early childhood who sometimes became physically ill in social situations, personal remembrance only points
up the amazing accuracy of his fictional portrayals. Good-look-
ing, kind, and gentle, Lionel was witty, sensitive, and artistic
like his mother. In village eyes, and his father's, he was a sissy.
Partly from nature, partly from nurture, Lionel was unable—
and unwilling—to take his place in life.

Elizabeth accepted her responsibility for her unhappy son and
suffered with him. Her family-centered late novels deal from
a woman's perspective with the unresolved tensions of her relations with Lionel, Paul, and Rosamund. Although a part of her
died with Lionel, she continued to do her duty, and her last
novel, *Late and Soon,* reveals her courageous resolution.

## Last Years

The last years of Elizabeth's life were overshadowed in every
way by the war. Her sadness was always there for those who
could see it, but she enjoyed to the end what there was to
enjoy.

These years were lightened by her friendship with Irish novelist Kate O'Brien, who loved Elizabeth and Croyle, and who
was much liked by the family. Kate alone saw Elizabeth as a
heroine, and her portrait of her friend in *That Lady* was accepted
as an essentially true picture of her.

Elizabeth seems to have experienced a renewal of affection
for Paul Dashwood as a friend and comrade. While their estrangement remained a reality, she also seems to have appreciated him in a way she had not before. She several times said
of him near the end of her life, "He can always surprise me
and make me laugh." The wife in a late BBC radio sketch,
"Middle-Aged Couple," observes at one point: "After romance
is over, companionship is still worth working for." This view
seems to have been Elizabeth's also.

She learned that she was terminally ill in the summer of 1943,
but she did not curtail her arduous schedule in any way. Kate
O'Brien remembers her gaily climbing her fig tree at Croyle
to pick and eat figs only weeks before her death. She collapsed
while lecturing at Oxford on 1 December 1943 and died at
home two days later.

While a world at war could only pause to pay homage to this talented, courageous, and patriotic woman, obituaries appeared in every English paper and in many throughout the English-speaking world. Her fellow judges on the Devon bench gave notice in a Bristol paper that "she had stood out as a magistrate, especially on the Bench of the Juvenile Court." She would have greatly liked that. A Requiem Mass was sung for her at St. James in London, and a large funeral cortege followed her coffin from Croyle to St. Mary's in Kentisbeare. Editorial letters in the weeks following expressed the sense of loss occasioned by the passing of the Provincial Lady. She was buried with Lionel where she always wished to be, under the great yew in the churchyard. Her inscription on the Dashwood tombstone reads, "A Clear Shining After Rain."

*Chapter Two*

# The Early Novels: 1917–23

E. M. Delafield's first fictional period includes nine novels published in seven years (1917–23). All nine deal with the maturational problems of girls or young women, and each in some way addresses a very old question: is the source of individual unhappiness located outside the self in heredity and environment, or does the ultimate responsibility reside with the individual?

Since it was only by trying to understand the trauma of her own troubled, near-tragic youth that she was able to proceed with her life and her art, Delafield struck her major subject matter early—domestic problems based on her family life. She rehearsed her own experience again and again in her fiction, projecting key events in a variety of ways in the effort to discover reasons for her early failures and unhappiness. Her youthful protagonists thus search in various ways for "reality" or "the bedrock of truth," and their situations all possess formal and thematic similarities.

First, the protagonist is an outsider, different in some way from those around her. A racial mixture or the offspring of parents from different social classes, she tends to be a Catholic and thus outside the mainstream of English life. Second, one or both of her parents are unloving, ineffective, or dead. She is either orphaned, or her father is vague and distant; her mother cold and critical. She craves for love and understanding but never receives them. Third, she is emotionally maladjusted, and her school years, social debut or entry into adulthood, and romantic life are disastrous.

Fourth, her craving for love—an obsessive desire for "an exclusive personal affection"—leads her to embrace religion when she feels shut out from human love. Finally, she realizes as an adult that her youth had nothing to do with "reality," that she is an emotionally stunted misfit unsuited for any useful activity.

All of these early bildungsroman project Delafield's own experience through psychological analyses of her protagonists, and their striking feature consists in the depth and intensity with which she probed her past. Characters, incidents, schools, houses—all can be matched with their real-life counterparts; but the autobiographical qualities of the first four novels make a tighter pattern within this group. In the three novels based on her childhood, Delafield cut each time more deeply into her past, and in *Consequences* she faced with searing biographical candor the emotional mess of her life up to her twenty-fourth year. Categorizing these works emphasizes their similarities and signals their position as direct contrasts to her last four novels, where Delafield focused again on her family—this time as mother rather than daughter.

## The Early Family Novels

*Zella Sees Herself,* Delafield's first novel, set the thematic pattern: the adult world's miseducation of a young woman whose romantic view of life fails to fit social reality. The five-point paradigm above may be taken as a plot summary of this novel, as Zella moves through girlhood, convent school, and into society trying unsuccessfully to conform to "type," while at the same time trying to discover "what is real." From early childhood, she finds herself at some crossroad—caught between child and adult, England and France, Protestant and Catholic, reality and convention. "Chameleon-like," Zella either adopts inauthentic roles or lies in order to meet the demands of these opposed worlds. Refusing to face the facts of any situation, or unaware of these facts, she invents her own. Thus, she is never quite sure what is true or real.

Although typical of the discursive, slow-paced romances of the day, *Zella* is solidly constructed and carefully characterized. Authorial distance insures a consistently ironic tone, and several chapters, notably the epistolary seventeenth, are technically fine.

But the chief reason for its favorable reception by both readers and reviewers lay in the characterization of Zella. Contrary to popular practice, Delafield resisted making a heroine; instead, Zella is a liar, a *poseuse.* While her family environments inhibit her development, Zella's egotism is responsible for her successive social failures. A dreamy, defensive romantic, Zella shuts herself off from real life, only to awake as an adult to the realization that a firm sense of reality is the prime requisite for living.

*The War Workers* continues Delafield's analysis of egotism, but it leaps over the protagonist's early years to focus on her adult present—paralleling the author's own present happiness and sense of purpose, which relegated to the background another novel based on her early life, eventually published (as *The Pelicans*) in the same year. *The War Workers* is an upbeat, even high-spirited account of Delafield's own war service, and is notable for its first hints of her comic gifts.

Headstrong, aristocratic Charmian Vivian serves as V.A.D. director of the Midland Supply Depot. Her long hours, close attention to detail, and haughty manner suggest a selfless devotion to duty that her enthralled staff struggles to emulate. But her imperiousness irritates her mother, especially when Char refuses to remain at home during her father's serious illness and when she brushes aside the attentions of Captain Trevellyan, whom her family expect her eventually to marry. Grace Jones, the sole critic among Char's worshipful staff, joins Lady Vivian in skeptically regarding Char as "the reincarnation of Queen Elizabeth." As the imperious director is examined from two points of view—selfless Miss Vivian at work and selfish Char the willful daughter at home—her friends and fellow workers are forced to decide what motivates her actions.

When Sir Piers Vivian dies and Char dismisses the kindly V.A.D. hostel manager, her egotism is clear to all. Trevellyan proposes to natural, human Grace Jones; Lady Vivian makes a convalescent home of her large country house; and Char, forced to seek rooms, is "brought to a gradual realization of motives in her own self-devotion hitherto unacknowledged to herself."[1]

The novel's main theme, then, echoes that of *Zella:* egotism is destructive to the egotist, who is not completely aware of her self-absorption and who creates tension in any situation. Conflict in this plot centers on character motivation, and plot complements theme through supporting characters' questions about Char's actions and the omniscient narrator's comments on these actions. As the novel opens, Char's staff discuss their chief as a woman of heroic mold, but immediately thereafter Lady Vivian pictures her daughter as being willful and head-

strong. When Char herself enters the novel, the narrator soon
alerts the reader that she is both. As we are always ahead of
the characters, dramatic irony operates throughout this novel.

While the novel contains a fine character study, its relevance
lies in its comic scenes. Delafield included a number of war
workers in the book, and without demeaning the war effort,
ridiculed a variety of phonies. Chief among them is Lesbia
Willoughby, a wealthy dowager who functions as a secondary
demonstration of egotism. Lesbia "billows" into the story and
immediately becomes a prime object of satire: "This war is killing me—simply killing me!" she shrieks. "Work is the only
thing! I must work or I shall go quite mad" (*WW*, 56). Her
idea of work turns out to be driving colonial officers around
London. "I make a speciality of South Africans," she confides,
"they're so delightfully rural" (*WW*, 25).

*The War Workers* contains a high percentage of dialogue in
comparison with the more serious novels of this group. Delafield
carefully set up her comic scenes and let her characters interact.
There is less of the intrusive narrator here than in any of the
early novels. Light, dramatic, topical—its humorous picture of
the home front was most welcome in 1918, and appreciative
reviewers compared her favorably with Jane Austen. Comedy,
however, had to wait upon the course of psychological analysis
through which she examined her formative years—an analysis
that continued in her next novel.

The orphaned Grantham sisters in *The Pelicans* are opposites:
Rosamund is rebellious, growing up "at odds with her world
and her passionate, unbalanced self." Francie, two years younger, is a dreamer for whom the material world scarcely exists.
The movement of this novel, while detailing Francie's steady
progress toward a religious vocation, primarily traces Rosamund's rites of passage from rebellious romantic egotist to realistic adult.

The main problem in Rosamund's psychological development
concerns her symbiotic relationship with Francie, whom she
mothers with passionate intensity. Other relationships are completely subordinate to this, and when Francie determinedly embraces Catholicism, enters a convent, and becomes a novice,
Rosamund experiences a crushing sense of rejection. Before
she can visit the convent, Francie dies, and Rosamund must
begin life anew, and alone.

She attains no romantic epiphany, but does reach an objective understanding of her past which allows her to live more deliberately. Her "intensely capable," that is, unromantic, cousin Bertie Tregaskis summarizes Rosamund's situation explicitly, and her assessment fits all of Delafield's confused young women: "All she needed was to find herself. . . . The child had to learn proportion. . . . Reality is the only medium for reality, after all. Her other emotions and phases weren't real you know. She had to get right down to bedrock to teach her what relative values are."[2]

By doubling her protagonists, both of whom are psychological doubles of herself, Delafield analyzed more deeply two paradoxical aspects of her own youthful character. Francie's religious story tallies with the known facts of Delafield's convent years: for instance, the large meals that neither Francie nor Edmeé de la Pasture could finish in the regulation twenty minutes, causing both to petition: "Ma mere, puis je aller finir au refectoire?"

And with striking candor, Delafield included a memorable event from her own convent experience, using what was probably her own convent name. In "Brides of Heaven," the novice decides to leave the convent when the novice mistress tears up a personal letter, throws the pieces on her bed, and refuses to allow her to rewrite it. In *The Pelicans,* Francie sees "Soeur Marie-Edmeé crying hysterically over the torn pieces of a letter laying on her desk." "Soeur Marie-Edmeé was impulsive and emotional, and very soon afterwards she had disappeared from the novitiate" (*P,* 106).

Through Rosamund, Delafield examined another case of youthful romanticism at odds with life. Rosamund is repeatedly burned by her excessive emotionalism and must seek the balm of common things. When she is "impersonal," that is, when she checks her egotism, she is charming; but she is frequently so excessively concerned with self that she expresses "a perfectly unconscious egotism," becoming distant, hostile, and uncommunicative. Like Zella, Rosamund at first appears to be a romantic heroine; but the reader soon learns that she needs to become more objective, to really *see* external reality and other people.

Alex Clare, the tragic protagonist of *Consequences,* never obtains an objective view of reality. The eldest daughter of Sir Francis and Lady Isobel, Alex seeks slavishly but unsuccessfully for affection throughout her nursery and school years. Her excessive behavior causes repeated humiliations at her convent, and in consequence her repressed emotions find sublimation in romantic dreams. She debuts at eighteen, unsuccessfully, and, when she cannot find love in the world, impulsively seeks to satisfy her emotional needs by entering a convent in Belgium.

Eight years later, Sister Alexandra's only attachment to life is her love for the mother superior; but when Mother Gertrude is posted to South America, Alex breaks down and asks to be relieved of her vows. In the nightmare which follows, all the guilty anxiety that made Alex a neurotic child returns in force. The interviewing priest denounces her for cheating God and assures her that she will be damned. Alex desperately persists, and the church finally releases her. She returns to England broken in mind and body.

An equally terrible nightmare ensues as Alex tries to resume her life in the world. Her poor health—she is emaciated and her teeth, hair, and skin are those of a woman twice her age—mirrors her spiritual and psychological condition. She cannot handle money, traffic, society, or any common aspect of daily life. She frightens and embarrasses her family, who cannot understand her: "Alex was embarrassed, too, a horrible feeling of failure and inadequacy crept over her. . . . It was the helpless insecurity of one utterly at variance with her surroundings" (*C,* 285).

To avoid further embarrassment to her family, Alex takes miserable lodgings, paying for them with a check her brother had left her for his servant's wages. To impress upon her the need for careful money-management, he later accuses her of embezzlement. Alex, crushed utterly, sees only one possibility for mending her situation. In the one successful act in her life of failure, she commits suicide.

*Consequences,* the most powerful of the early family novels, climaxes Delafield's first fictional analyses of her formative years. Unhappy, neurotic, and purposeless at age twenty-four, her life really began when she became E. M. Delafield the novelist, a persona with the freedom to acquire new perspectives. War work gave her self-confidence, and she began to trace that "pattern of conversion" so often found in the works of her favorite Victorians, in which the Everlasting No gradually gives way to the Everlasting Yea. Like Thomas Carlyle, Elizabeth had experienced the worst that life could offer, had withstood it, and had begun to use her past positively as an artist.

## From the Malay States

Her next four novels show that although she still drew heavily on her own life, she could control and shape that experience into fiction more objectively than before. That none of these books justifies the promise of the first four may be attributed to several factors: marriage, the move to Hong Kong, Lionel's birth. Next to nothing is known of her life during these years, and—for whatever reason—her next books seem derivative, abstract, cut off from life. As memories of England blurred, so did the freshness of her writing. She remained aloof from both native life and British society, unwilling or unable to integrate herself into her new environment. A little of her colonial experience found its way into her journalism later, but she never found a place for it in her novels—a strange situation, considering the wealth of British colonial literature.

In contrast to the early family novels, Delafield gives answers here instead of asking questions. *Tension* is a good-humored romance on the Victorian "second-best" model. Pauline Marchrose's jilting of one suitor and romance with a married man affront local convention, in the person of neighborhood grande dame Lady Rossiter. Marchrose is hounded from her college position; but she accepts the proposal of a colleague, and the pair set out for the East as educational pioneers. Dedicated with terse irreverence "To My Maternal Parent," Delafield caricatures her mother in Lady Rossiter. Caricature is the dominant mode in this, her most Dickensian work; and on one level, characters are judged by whether or not they appreciate the Great Boz.

*Tension,* with its unbelievable love story, its Dickensian caricatures and subplots, should be seen as a comic blast at conventional social authority, a metaphor for Delafield's triumph over them. Like Marchrose, Delafield had at last escaped the dominance of the grande dame and sailed away with her comrade "to the colonies."

*Humbug,* following a negligible study of egotism in *The Heel*

*of Achilles,* criticizes adult society again for hiding the truth from
its youth, thus causing them to lose touch with reality. Lily
Stellenthorpe grows up under the tutelage of "amateur educationalists" who systematically stifle her intellectual growth by
repressing every honest thought or emotion she has. These ama-
teurs are Lily's parents, who like her to call them Phillip and
Eleanor, and whose typical response to her is "Don't ask foolish
questions, my little pet." At eighteen, Lily finds life with her
doll more real than any relationship she has with "all those
Real Life People."

The epithet "amateur educationalists" symbolizes all adults
in this novel, and Lily does not begin to grow up until she
discovers her husband's infidelity. Although the amateur educationalists beseige her with advice, Lily finds for the first time
that she can control her own life: divorce, separation, reconcilia-
tion—all decisions affecting her are in her hands, and the narrator informs us that "she had learned honesty at last." Lily has
learned that parental authority which stifles intellectual and emotional growth in youth by passing along stale convention as
truth is a humbug, a category in this novel which includes most
of the adult world.

The *Optimist* pits a cynical World War I veteran, Owen Quentillian, against the Victorian optimist, Canon Morchard. The
canon seems to have sprung full-blown from the pages of Robert
Browning in his belief that God's in his heaven and all's right
with the world. Quentillian opposes the canon's principles to
the point of writing against them; his article, "The Myth of
Self-Sacrifice," has been well-received in London.

Against this background of dissension between old and new
viewpoints, the disposition of the five Morchard children provides plot conflict. None can live by their father's principles;
all suffer from his dominance. One repressed and neurotic
daughter chooses to become "as the beautiful old devotional
phrase has it, 'The Bride of Heaven,' " and dies in a convent.

But what sets out to be another criticism of establishment
views doubles back upon itself as the reflector character, Quentillian, changes his mind about Canon Morchard. Whereas at first
the canon "reminded him oddly of a book of late Victorian
memoirs," Quentillian comes to idolize the old man. The novel's
long discussions concerning the grounds of belief boil down

to two choices: hard facts and resignation or baseless hopes and seemingly facile optimism. Quentillian finally cannot decide, and the novel trails off into a Victorian ending of easy means with the unlikely marriage of Quentillian and the canon's oldest daughter.

*The Optimist,* dedicated to C. A. Dawson-Scott, feminist founder of the P.E.N. Club, is the last of Delafield's "colonial" books. They are all slightly fuzzy, talkily philosophical, and lack a firm sense of place.

## Themes and Techniques

The novels of Delafield's first period reveal a unity of focus and development of vision which are enriched by recurring themes and situations. All deal with young protagonists who struggle with conventional beliefs and attitudes in their search for some realistic basis for living. Although their goals are similar, each case remains distinctive—as seen by the conceptual terms used to describe it. The need for "proportion," "perspective," above all a "personal relationship" (love), urges these protagonists to battle with their environments.

Although the protagonists' situations inhibit their successful development, they themselves must at some point take responsibility for their lives. Here Delafield's great understanding of the Victorians received validation from her reading in modern psychology. At the storm center of modern life still lurked the ego.

George Meredith held that modern man's history could be traced by following "the Stench of Egoism" (the phrase is Dr. Shrapnel's in *Beauchamp's Career*), and his work, well-known to Delafield, effectively glosses the main theme of her first period. Meredith perceived two forms of the "disease": *egoism* proper and a milder form, *sentimentalism.* The milder form helps explain Delafield's egotists, who are marked by their "willful refusal to face unpleasant or brutal facts, [their] assumption of refined sensibility."[3]

Both her life and her reading had convinced Delafield that egotism in women was neurosis, and she located the disease primarily in the self. Susceptibility to this "disease" is inherent and exhibits itself—were any trained to see it—in early childhood. Young women are especially vulnerable because their romantic self-absorption leads them away from life rather than toward it. Immaturity, inexperience, and egocentric willfulness combine to spread the disease until it becomes fatal to happiness. Family, religion, school, peer pressure all contribute to its virulence, but environment remains a secondary cause. One sees the world as it is or one doesn't. As Bertie Tregasksis says of Rosamund Grantham's dawning appreciation of real life, "reality is the only medium for reality."

Delafield conceptualized straightforwardly what she saw as the main problems of young women. Translated into thematic terms, these are (1) the tendency toward romantic egotism, and (2) "the conflicts of motive within the individual, the unidentified urges and destructive frustrations that arise from conforming to artificial codes of conduct and accepting false standards of value."[4]

But the thematic articulation of egotism's destructiveness kept pace with her own developing views. As she came to understand the character flaws that marred her youth, she grew more critical of her romantic, egotistical protagonists. Her reaction against "artifical codes of conduct" and "false standards of value" modified as well, so that her dominant theme gradually engaged a number of other concerns or subthemes.

*The Optimist* provides a good example of Delafield's development in that her liberal and conservative views clash head-on. Problems of belief become fundamental in this novel as some resolution of the Quentillian / Canon Morchard conflict of ideas becomes necessary. Cynical Quentillian believes that optimism is "merely a veil drawn across the nakedness of Truth," but also sees that his own pessimism leads nowhere. Like young Wordsworth, he yields up moral questions in despair, and this collapse of the novel's dialectic reveals Delafield's own perplexity. Always troubled by problems of belief, postwar cynicism seemed to her as false a standard of value as unquestioning reverence of parents. Especially troubling was the problem of personal freedom, the conflict between duty to others and duty to self—in this novel's terms, "living a life of one's own" as opposed to "the Myth of Self Sacrifice."

Delafield engaged her major themes early and intensely. Conflicts over self, other, convention, belief, and duty form the bases for all of her fiction. Not until her last novel, in the year of her death, did she really resolve them.

Delafield's early work shows everywhere her indebtedness to Victorian models—at two levels. On the one hand, her concern with character, her thematic earnestness, her ironic tone and manner of narration all show her to be an heiress of what Frank Leavis has called the "Great Tradition." On the other hand, she was very concerned with the inner experience of being a woman, and her debt to minor women novelists like Charlotte Mary Yonge is a large one.

The conduct of these novels follows inevitably from three principles. First, Delafield was a creator of characters. Her interest in analysis of motivation never wavered, and she meticulously studied her protagonists—or two protagonists as antithetical sides of one self. In dedicating one novel to a psychologist friend, she articulates her credo clearly: causes are more interesting than the most dramatic results; strong action is merely accessory to the main issue, "which lies on that more subtle plane of thought where only personalities are deserving of dissection."[5]

Her characters tend to be types. She envisioned a type as a bundle of emotional and intellectual attributes that produced certain responses to situations in life. Paradoxically, these complex women must struggle against "conforming to type," that is, they must struggle against convention to achieve selfhood. Although her range of characterization seems narrow, she worked originally within it, and from her earliest reviews was praised for her "psychological studies."

Next, thematic seriousness dictated that each novel examine a central situation closely in order to elicit some experiential truth. Her serious work always proceeds from a closely held concept. The bias tends to be didactic and polemical, events tend to be illustrative, and narration outweighs dramatization.

Finally, Delafield adopts an omniscient point of view. Allied to deep character analysis and thematic seriousness, her use of omniscience leads to various kinds of summary and intrusiveness. On occasion the narrative voice assumes a pedagogical tone approaching moralizing.

She did utilize a reflector character in *The Optimist;* but even here the narrator intrudes. Although she would continue to experiment with different methods of narration, the objective,

ironic narrator remained her forte. This was design, not chance.
She disliked modern technical innovation and wrote: "I can't
bear the Dorothy Richardson method. The more I see of it,
the more I dislike it."[6] Always the realist, she was faulted, ironically, for being too understandable.

A typical pattern in a Delafield novel, whether early or late,
first "sets" the protagonist by means of a preliminary scene
that symbolizes her inner life. This scene is several times referred
to as a "keynote" even though Delafield understood symbolic
technique and used the term "symbol." The business of the
novel was then to examine each aspect of her protagonist's response to the keynote scene, generally by subjecting her to
contrasting character types representative of other, antithetical,
modes of experience. Typically, the early novels reveal similarities in structure; three of them, for instance, are thirty chapters
long. And they tend to have two movements: the first analyzes
character as above; the second forces a climax by subjecting
the protagonist to a situation she is not prepared to handle
and then studies her reactions.

The sensitive, paradoxically ironic sophistication of the authorial voice makes these novels work. The omniscient narrator
constructs a sympathetic characterization of the protagonist
through choice and presentation of scene, interior views, social
action, and comment; but also stays well ahead of the character(s)
and keeps sufficient distance to allow for the full play of irony.
The narrator's sympathy results, of course, from the fact that
her protagonists' situations often drew deeply on her own. Her
irony stems from her recognition that romantic self-absorption
was inimical to normal development.

At its best, Delafield's technique led to a powerful novel
like *Consequences,* where narrative control produced a claustrophobic, Hardyesque atmosphere that recalls the story of "predes-
tinate Jude." *Consequences* is told in the past tense, symbolic of
Alex's predestined end. Alex never gains her balance in the
present. Past failures obviate any chance of present success for
this character, whose weakly impulsive nature causes her always
to react emotionally. Past perfect tenses and additive sentence
structure often swamp even the simple past, locking Alex into
"a plane of existence" which precludes any possibility of choice
or change.

With these early novels, Delafield launched and solidified her reputation. In them a patent emotional confusion gives way gradually to clarity as she unified her work around the theme of egotism and worked against her romantic instincts. Marriage, the Dashwood's move to the East, and the birth of her son helped to create the distance necessary for a new perspective. While she clung to family subjects, present events gradually loosened the hold of the past. When the family returned to England in 1922, Elizabeth had changed.

## Chapter Three

# The Novels of Midcareer: 1924–29

The more experimental novels of midcareer mark this period as a time of trial and error. Although her chief experiments had to do with subject matter, Delafield also tried different methods of storytelling. She moved beyond her Victorian models and considerably streamlined her typical novelistic form. Instead of her usual pattern—exposition, rendered scene, and authorial comment—she tended to replace chapter expositions with dialogue openings, constructed tighter, more dramatic scenes, used dialogue instead of narration, reduced authorial intrusion, and modified the omniscient point of view.

While these eight novels are not as thematically unified as those in her first period, they all deal with the same subject. If the key question in her first novels is, what is truth?—representing an attempt to distinguish reality from conventional humbug—the question here can be taken from the title of one of them: *What Is Love?* In each novel, Delafield examines aspects of modern love in much the same way as she had examined family life, working through her own experience toward understanding and acceptance. Her examination of love generally transcends the personal experience on which it was based; with one notable exception, she tried to project her experience more imaginatively and reduced the element of biography.

Most importantly, she left a record in these novels of an intelligent woman's response to postwar social mores. Delafield returned from the sleepy Far East to a country frantically pursuing "The Long Week-end." In their book of that title, Robert Graves and Alan Hodge note that "The Careless Twenties" saw such phenomena as nudity, homosexuality, Freudianism, and relativity burst into public discussion.[1] Delafield, like most of her countrywomen, was hit by this wave of future shock, and her fictional response to it seems representative. She criticized many postwar fads, but she was mainly concerned that her society's new obsession with sex threatened traditional forms of love.

Delafield's pervasive concern with what she referred to as "the personal element" remained basic to her view of life. The one necessity in life she had learned, even before her convent years, was loving companionship. Her own difficulty in establishing love relationships and her never-ending desire for them are reflected again and again in her novels. The protagonists of the early novels fail to a woman to achieve romantic love, and they are equally unsuccessful in relationships with parents, siblings, and friends. Thus, the Victorian second-best syndrome is ubiquitous: the best these young women can do is to accept the older man who befriends them during their difficult periods of growing up. But these dim Platonic relationships are rejected in Delafield's novels of the mid and late twenties, where the chaste kiss gives way to "magnetism," and sexual desire is fully recognized.

## Modern Love

Delafield's reentry into English society first produced a potboiler, *A Reversion to Type,* which makes a plea for greater understanding of mental illness in children. It deals with congenital lying as a disease that passes from father to son, and it was instrumental in Delafield's appointment as justice of the peace for Devonshire in 1925. *Reversion* is a transition novel, reflecting again its author's lifelong interest in children; and her enlightened viewpoint elicited some good reviews. Its male protagonist and lack of direct biographical material show her developing objectivity also, but this novel's old-fashioned plotting and talkiness mark it a failure.

Delafield's reaction to postwar sexual mores really begins with the sensational *Messalina of the Suburbs,* where for the first time she projected herself into a character totally unlike her own. *Messalina* appeared soon after the execution of Edith Jesse Thompson and Frederic Bywater for the murder of Edith's husband. The still classic Bywater-Thompson case created front-page news for months in England, and its elements seem made

to order for Delafield: the repressed passion of a literate, romantic woman leading to a tragic end.

Her psychological "reconstruction," as she called it, presented
her protagonist as the victim of sexual determinism. Elsie Palmer's sexual precocity results from the attentions paid her by
her mother's boarders, and soon "physical arousal" creates the
only excitement in her life. Elsie's extreme sexuality leads directly to murder in Delafield's analysis; and in her fictional equa-
tion, romantic temperament plus physical susceptibility equals
destruction. This linking of physical passion and tragedy recurs
in her novels, and it forms the thesis in her dialectical discussion
of modern love.

Delafield continued her inquiry into the physical side of love
in *The Chip and the Block.* Paul Ellery, the central protagonist
of this rambling novel, finds in the arms of his landlady, Mrs.
Foss, salvation from a false, sentimental attachment. This vital
widow listens to unawakened Paul recount the kinds of emotional blackmail Gladys St. Lawrence and her manipulative
mother use to get him to propose, and then convinces him
that Gladys does not love him. If she did, Mrs. Foss declares,
she would show it. Thereupon, she turns out the light, and
her "shapely outline" shows prominently through her red frock
as she stands in front of the fire. Paul "woke, suddenly and
violently, to the fact that she was physically desirable."

A typographical break disposes of the time during which Paul
and Mrs. Foss (now "Marga") develop "entirely new relations,"
and the omniscient narrator immediately places Paul's epiphany
in perspective, understanding his "lack of niceness" while still
not condoning it: "There was a certain link between them, although it was not of a high spiritual order, and he somehow
felt that their connection was, on the whole, less of an offense
against sincerity than had been his entirely platonic affair with
Gladys St. Lawrence."[2]

This passage is Delafield's most liberal pronouncement on
sex, and as it is without parallel in her work, it must take all
of the interpretative weight it can bear. The key terms here
are "offense" and "spiritual." And the narrator heavily qualifies
her guarded response: "certain," "although," "somehow," "on
the whole," "less of." What Delafield does here is recognize
the honesty of the sex drive but rank it lower than spiritual
love.

She carefully limits the situation: unmarried Paul has not se-
duced the widow; it is tea and sympathy all the way. Marga
tells him matter-of-factly that sex is merely a matter of temperament. Some women like sex she says, adding that there is no
reason "to fuss" if no one else is hurt. Still, Paul has offended,
has given into his animal nature and settled for something less
than a spiritual relationship.

Marga's temperament is not like her creator's, nor does the
novel emphasize her view. For example, Paul's sister ruins her
life with an affair. But while the liberal views of this minor
character provide only a minority opinion, no other fictional
woman in Delafield's work speaks so frankly and with such
freedom. Moreover, the narrator endorses her position as Paul's
savior.

The central situation in this novel, then, Paul's sexual awaken-
ing, should be viewed as a serious exercise in definition. Delafield's dismay at finding her countrymen seemingly obsessed
with sex upon her return from the East worked itself out in
her fiction. Her women characters do feel a good deal of sexual
pressure, but not from men. There are almost no predatory
males in her novels. Rather, her women feel pressured from
without by convention on the one hand and postwar permissiveness on the other. But it is the internal demands of their romantic
desires conflicting with sexual fears that troubles them most.
The point of view in these novels is primarily that of the middle-
class woman, and these women are subject to a crushing weight
of inhibition.

While female flirtatiousness falls within the limits of good
breeding, unless a woman is of the Elsie Palmer type, sexual
fastidiousness is the rule for Delafield's women, and this antithesis in her love-sex dialectic is represented by a recurring character type who is not highly sexed. These characters' inhibitions
vary in degree, but they always manifest an essential chastity
that puts them at odds with the sexual mores of their time.
They are suspicious of passion, even when it goes hand-in-hand
with love, and most of the women in the novels of this period
conform to this type.

The epitome is Cathie Galbraith, a negative demonstration
of theme in *Jill,* who tries hardest to understand the title character. Cathie's obsession with cleanliness is blatantly anal, and
her fastidiousness is linked with her lack of passion. She covers

her undergarments when her husband Oliver enters her bedroom, finds talk of birth and babies distasteful (her own baby is stillborn), and recoils from Jill's open-armed embracing of life. The narrator poses her problem clearly in mid-story during a discussion of Jill's passionate vitality: "Cathie, who was temperamentally frigid, and who rather disliked being touched than otherwise, suddenly wished violently that her husband should kiss her."[3]

Cathie's sexual fastidiousness and her doubts about her sexual attractiveness are echoed by a number of Delafield's women characters. And they certainly reflect strong personal feelings of the author, who had herself been a beautiful young woman, but by age twenty-eight had received only one proposal—from unemotional, unromantic Paul Dashwood. She was still accounted beautiful ten years later, but friends recall that she did not have "it." She was attractive but also inexperienced and unawakened. Whatever her sex drive, she lacked confidence and gave no evidence of that "magnetism" that so interested her in these novels.

Although Cathie and Oliver lead a culturally rich existence, unaffected by England's depression, their unpassionate, well-arranged marriage reveals itself as a sterile denial of life and love. Their opposites, Oliver's cousin Jack and his wife Doreen, lead equally sterile lives. Both are victims of the war, "without joy, without morals, and without hope." They live for the moment, hand-to-mouth, and their marriage amounts only to an acquisitive partnership in which they cadge small amounts of goods, credit, or money—Jack from small schemes, Doreen from male admirers.

The money theme in this novel is the same as in Dickens or Thackeray. In the demimondaine world of Jack and Doreen, money has replaced love and moral principle as life's goal. The con-artist Jack becomes involved with believes only in money: "*nothing* else is any good in this world."

Jill, the symbolic title character, emerges as Delafield's first heroine. Her mother is a kept woman who relinquishes Jill first to Jack and Doreen and then to Cathie and Oliver, but none of the perversions of love which mark her three environments can touch her. She stands for joy, vitality, and purity; and when Jack has divorced himself from the sterile amorality represented by Doreen, Jill marries him. Like other of her romantic couples, Delafield rewards them with a new life out East.

*Jill* is a polished tract for the times, a fable critical of the thrill-seeking, money-hungry, live-for-the-moment pop culture of the day that Delafield found repellent. She intended to lift the concept of love above the amorality and cynicism of the twenties, and in this romance found a place for pure, spiritual love.

Delafield summarizes fictionally her love/sex dialectic in *Jill.* Her thesis that excessive sexuality is destructive reinforces her treatment of Elsie Palmer in *Messalina.* While the "certain link" between Paul and Marga in *The Chip and the Block* proves to be more honest than sentiment, it lacks the spiritual quality necessary for love. The antithesis is Cathie's frigidity, a denial of life. Only through romantic love—symbolized by the pure love of Jill—could Delafield find a synthesis.

Of the four other novels of this period, three add nothing either to Delafield's inquiry into modern love or to her reputation. *Mrs. Harter* is a tragedy of star-crossed lovers. *What is Love* ironically contrasts traditional and modern love through two cousins, one a romantic "Sleeping Princess" who cannot see reality, and the other a smart, self-confident modern. Only two years after *Jill,* Delafield could find no realistic basis for romantic love. *The Suburban Young Man,* her second novel in 1928, is one which she always regretted writing.

The remaining novel of this group is the best of her first sixteen, and it deserves fuller discussion.

## *The Way Things Are*

*The Way Things Are* shows E. M. Delafield nearly at her best. This milestone in her career exhibits her keen wit; its control of an ironic point of view, which was becoming her trademark, and fine dramatic scenes, concision, and deft pacing represent a considerable advance. Delafield caught the modern note perfectly in this realistic social satire; and although it is autobiographical, it rises above the personal as the protagonist's situation assumes general significance. For the first time in her career, her insight, her historical moment, and her art as novelist join to produce a first-rate work.

*The Way Things Are* is her first novel to justify reviewers'

comparisons with Jane Austen's writing. Light, bright, and sparkling throughout, the ironies of domestic life play about the
heroine as well as about those she associates with, and the rich
incongruities of her inner thoughts and feelings as these clash
with her social world make for a succession of fine satires of
circumstance. Like Austen, Delafield discriminates between attitudes in a phrase, and the nineteen chapters of the novel remind
one of nothing so much as one of the nineteen-chapter volumes
of *Pride and Prejudice.*

Laura Fairchild—married seven years to a gentleman farmer,
mother of two little boys, mistress of a country house, sometime
writer—fears that she is becoming a vegetable. She feels middle-
aged, unromantic, depressed, and completely trapped. She realizes daily that "from being a bright young mother in the morning, she had degenerated into a whining victim by the evening."
Family life "reduces her to physical pulp and spiritual
exhaustion."[4] Though her middle-class life seems outwardly secure and successful, inwardly Laura feels it to be full of struggle,
conflict, and failure.

At the heart of her discontent stands unromantic, unresponsive, utterly conventional Alfred Temple, Delafield's first and
definitive portrait in a novel of the boringly insensitive husband.
Alfred seldom talks to Laura; when he does, it is only to utter
trenchantly conservative political opinions in a way that throttles
conversation. He is never, never personal. His only dealings
with his children consist of silencing them when they make a
noise. His one hobby seems to be weeding in the garden, at
which he does not like to be disturbed. Laura does not understand these "agricultural proclivities" which Alfred so obviously
relishes—or indeed anything else about his emotionally tepid
and mechanical responses to living.

Alfred's habits have become Laura's pet peeves, which she
grimly but unsuccessfully tries to overlook—like his snoring
after dinner, or his inveterate habit of departing to prepare
for meals only after they have been announced. After dinner,
Alfred generally hides behind his paper, even in company, and
begins to doze: "They listened [to their guest], and Alfred appeared to listen also—but after a little while he began, by degrees, and with a certain effect of absentmindedness, to obtain
possession of *The Times,* behind which he gradually vanished,
presumably still listening, but perhaps less intently" ( *W,* 87).

Duke Ayland, a London music arranger, arrives to lighten Laura's boredom. Duke notices both Laura's inferiority complex and her inner beauty; he talks to her, personally, about herself; and he likes to touch her. He is a thrilling antithesis, and when domestic business calls Laura to London, the two meet daily and fall deeply in love. At their first kiss, "blindness and ecstasy descended upon her."

The novel's subplots interweave skillfully with the love story. All impinge upon the conflict between conventional marriage and "the New Sexual Freedom." In every social group Laura meets with in London, the "New Ideals" seem to prevail. These hold that everyone is abnormal, that the only abnormalities worth discussing are those concerned with sex, and that these cannot be discussed exhaustively enough. For instance, near the end of one comic scene, a psychopathic psychiatry student named Losh tramples all over Laura's reticence about sex. He concludes thus: " 'You're abnormal—I'm abnormal. Only we have it under control. . . .' Laura, gazing at him not without fascination, felt inclined to wonder whether we had" ( *W,* 285).

In another subplot, Laura watches the progress of popular writer A. B. Onslow, whose path several times crosses Laura's in London. At one of their meetings, talk veers round to Laura's last published story, and she feels that she is impressing him. But Bebee, a cigarette-smoking, heavily madeup young swinger in a jump suit, joins them.

It was at this point that Mr. Onslow's attention to his conversation with Laura, although it did not waver, gave her an impression of being, as it were, nailed to the mast, by courtesy and kind-heartedness.

Mrs. Temple, as an instant result, ceased to be either entertaining or responsively intelligent. . . . ( *W,* 44)

The Laura to Mrs. Temple switch typifies Delafield's skill in nuancing her heroine's objective and subjective roles, and both scenes illustrate her structural skill in selecting suitable character foils to challenge Laura's moral positions. Bebee represents the novel's reductio ad absurdum of sexual freedom; and Laura watches in astonishment as Bebee relentlessly separates Onslow from his wife on the grounds that he owes it to his work not to turn his back on love.

These recurrent collisions with the new ideals confuse Laura.

She loves Duke desperately and wishes to elope with him. But her honesty, her children, the seventh commandment, Alfred's essential goodness—rather a lot of moral imperatives—line up to block her path to freedom. Her desire for emotional satisfaction is incompatible with her sense of duty, and although she cannot end her affair she knows that it is over. Her last emotion-charged but beautifully ironic meeting with Duke takes place at a department store during the few moments she has while Alfred looks at water pumps. As Laura opens her mouth to reply to Duke's insistence that she run away with him, the waitress suddenly interrupts with the tea things, breaking the spell with her impersonal question: "Bleck or whayte?"

This is the way things are—black or white—there are no intermediate positions possible. Although nothing has been settled between herself and Duke, Laura knows that the moment of renunciation has passed. She and Duke must live "in common with the vast majority of their fellow-beings incapable of the ideal, imperishable, love for which the world was said to be well lost" (W, 335).

Laura's opportunity for romance ends with much the same whimper that concludes her typical day as a mother. But her concluding reflections stress her representative role and her philosophical acceptance of life as it is:

> Imagination, emotionalism, sentimentalism. . . . What woman is not the victim of these insidious and fatally unpractical qualities?
> But how difficult, Laura reflected, to see oneself as an average woman and not, rather, as one entirely unique, in unique circumstances. . . .
> It dawned upon her dimly that only by envisaging and accepting her own limitations, could she endure the limitations of her surroundings. (W, 336)

Biographical fact saturates this novel, allowing an inside view of how Delafield and women of her class lived in the mid-1920s. The emotional record of her marriage is truly set forth here: Alfred is Paul Dashwood. Laura's reasons for marrying, for dissatisfaction with marriage, and for remaining faithful to her husband were Delafield's. So too were the problems of housewife and mother. The constant clash in Laura's life between dulling domestic duties and social obligations and the need for romance, for her own time and space, was Delafield's principal problem in mid-career.

Thoughtful, insightful, and accurate, *The Way Things Are* is an important document in the history of women's literature. With its themes of entrapment and renunciation, it is in many ways an angry book, a compelling full-length portrait of an intelligent, sensitive woman chained to deadening domesticity. At one point, for example, the only bright spot in Laura's week is a planned lunch date with Duke. But though she tries desperately to keep these few hours free, in the end domesticity wins. Laura's sense of helpless frustration over her inability to control even small aspects of her life strikes a chord that has become loud and dissonant with the women's movement.

Similarly, the weighing of new forms of social/sexual freedom against the ties that bind husband and wife together after romantic love dies anticipates the fear of flying so prevalent in contemporary fiction. The unromantic synthesis Delafield reaches shows her concern for maintaining the family unit despite postwar attacks on the social fabric. She accepts flatly that "the things of respectability keep one respectable," and reaches this matter-of-fact conclusion inductively; both sides of the will-she-or-won't-she debate are seriously prosecuted, but also presented with a wit and wisdom achievable only by a quick intelligence alert to the incongruities inherent in life as it is.

The conservative conclusion demanded by moral respectability represents more than a Victorian ending of easy means, however. Laura's pruning out of romance and her acceptance of things as they are continue Delafield's criticism of subjective responses to life. The message of the family novels remains the same: women must not retreat into "imagination, emotionalism, sentimentalism"; they must remain in the world and view it clearly and objectively.

Plot, character, theme, tone, and language coalesce into a finished performance in *The Way Things Are*. We never leave Laura's consciousness, and she is a perfect point of view character. While her naiveté is genuine, it repeatedly sets up situations in which the time-lag of satire flourishes. Always a little behind in comprehension, a little wide-eyed and rigid, a bit breathless and bruised by the series of small defeats in the satires of circumstance in which she must take part, Laura is never self-indulgent.

Like Elizabeth Bennet, her principles and her common sense see her through. She is a wholly successful character with whom it is impossible not to laugh at, sympathize with, and care for. She points directly ahead to the Provincial Lady, that famous persona equally close to Delafield herself.

## Chapter Four

# The Journalism: 1923–39

E. M. Delafield's popular reputation, a considerable one by the early thirties, received a great boost from her work in journalism. Her male readership, for instance, tended to make her acquaintance in the pages of *Punch* rather than in her novels; whereas the intellectual woman was as likely to know her work from *Time and Tide* as from her fiction. While she wrote for more than a dozen periodicals, the bulk of her journalism, and most of the best, appeared in these two magazines.

Delafield published at least one article every week in some major magazine for about fifteen years. This represents quite a level of production for a housewife active in local civic affairs, who also wrote novels and plays, and who made lecture tours and radio broadcasts at home and abroad. And the best of this work is of high quality. At her death, Delafield's distinctive form of the comic sketch, over the initials E. M. D., was a widely recognized trademark; her persona, the Provincial Lady, a household term. It will be the purpose of this chapter to recall this all-but-forgotten aspect of her talent by tracing her development into one of England's finest, most famous journalists.

## *Time and Tide:* 1922–32

The story of Delafield's celebrated rise to the top of her field goes back to 1922. She turned to magazine writing for obvious reasons: she needed money. Newly back from the Malay States, the Dashwoods found England sinking into economic depression. Major Dashwood had given up his career to please his wife and could not find suitable employment at home. He never did. The family settled in Devon, and setting up a home commensurate with their station required a steadier income than novel writing could provide.

She chose her primary journal wisely. *Time and Tide* was barely

two years old. Founded by Vicountess Margaret Rhondda as
an intellectual feminist journal, it rapidly developed under her
astute leadership into one of England's leading literary and political magazines. Lady Rhondda recalled later that when Elizabeth
began to write for the magazine, it was not yet on a firm financial
footing, and that her contributions were significant in making
it economically sound. Eventually many distinguished persons
on both sides of the Atlantic contributed. Virginia Woolf, Vita
Sackville-West, Edith Sitwell, Rebecca West, Winifred Holtby,
Katherine Mansfield, and Sylvia Townsend Warner were among
the brilliant women whose work appeared in its pages. And
the likes of George Bernard Shaw (who contributed without
payment whenever asked), H. G. Wells, E. M. Forster, and
St. John Ervine wrote for it with some regularity as well. It
was quite a heady company for the shy Devonshire housewife.

*Time and Tide* began publication on 14 May 1920; Delafield
began as a book reviewer on 5 May 1922, replacing Rose Macau-
lay who shared reviewing chores on alternating weeks with another novelist, Mary Agnes Hamilton. Delafield's biweekly
reviews are mainly appreciative, as might be expected from
an inveterate novel reader. She was critical of faulty psychological motivation and wooden dialogue, but her best reviews are
generous and well-written, as for instance her praise of F. Scott
Fitzgerald's *The Beautiful and the Damned.*[1]

With the acceptance of her first article, late in 1923, she
gave up regular reviewing to concentrate on original, higher
paid work more congenial to her talents—although she occasionally reviewed books of particular interest to her for *Time
and Tide* throughout the rest of her life. She made her way
gradually into the inner circle of the magazine, through stories
and articles expressing the complexities of the feminine viewpoint.

## Feminine Bias

The feminist bias, so evident in her journalism, stemmed as
usual from her own family life, as in the short story, "Appreciation," for 24 May 1924, which dealt with marital incompatibil-
ity.

Caroline was unhappily married.

Freddie was quite happily married.

Unfortunately for Caroline, it was to one another that they were married.

A singular daydream had obsessed Caroline for many years. Summarized, it amounted to a Public Recognition of her merits, to take place in the presence of Freddie.

Caroline's poetry *has* received recognition from the *Times Literary Supplement;* but Freddie, unfortunately, has read neither the *Supplement* nor the poetry. What recognition Caroline gets from him consists of a catalog of her failings. Especially irritating, Freddie constantly reiterates that she never notices anything: "One of the few personal remarks that he ever made to her, Freddie made often. 'I suppose you're about as unobservant as they make 'em, old thing. It's really extraordinary.' "

Caroline's interests, "not being tangible things," and Freddie's never coincide; but after ten years, her moment arrives. They are invited to meet a Frenchman so distinguished that even Freddie recognizes his name.

The great man admired Caroline's poetry. He admired it out loud, publicly, in front of Freddie, in front of everybody. He quoted some of Caroline's verses, and raved about them.

Amongst other things he said—and his voice was what is known as a "carrying" one—that Caroline's powers of observation amounted to genius.

Powers of observation!

Caroline nearly weeps with pride but worries about this shock to Freddie's ego and wonders how he will atone for a decade's obtuseness. Freddie, however, does not allude to the incident; and Caroline, tense and trembling, must broach the subject.

"So he—he's read my books, Freddie. Did you hear what he said?"

"Of course I heard what he said, dear. Everyone did, for that matter. I suppose that was the foreign idea of good manners. They're all alike greasy bounders."

Freddie yawned.

"Did you notice what an uncommonly good ice-pudding that was tonight?"

Caroline replied by a sound of some kind.

"Sorry, old girl," said Freddie, quite affectionately. "I forgot, you never *do* notice anything."

This ironic little story may be considered prototypic. We have already met Freddie—as Alfred Temple—and will meet him again under a variety of names. The opposed expectations of husband and wife, his strange mixture of affection and complete insensitivity—such satiric penetration into social incongruities typifies Delafield's journalism; and her subtle nuancing of the smallest psychological or sociological detail concerning women rapidly won her an enthusiastic readership.

## The Perfect "Light"

Complementing her popular feminist perspective, "E. M. Delafield was the perfect provider of good 'lights,' and as every editor knows, there is nothing so rare."[2] The writer of lights, continues this editor, does not attempt belles lettres, which would be out of place in magazine journalism. Even "the most perfect short story ever written is seldom in its absolutely right place in the pages of a weekly review." Rather, the perfect light applies brilliant technique to current subjects. "E. M. Delafield . . . had the most delicate sense for the exact flavour of the mood of the moment," and she became one of a handful of perfect lights—"topical, hot, perfect for the week."

"Progress," a typical early light article, concerns Auntie's dream; its generative mechanism is Delafield's favorite rhetorical topic, past versus present. In the past, dreams made humorous subjects for conversation, but since Freud's work the sexual nature of dream materials is well known. So, when poor old Auntie mentions that in her dream the previous night she stood by the sea, "her youngest nephew nods. Evidently he'd expected no less. 'The sea always symbolizes the Unconscious, of course,' he murmurs gravely." And when Auntie mentions that in her dream the tide was in flood, a married niece (modern) blushes. Auntie presses ahead desperately, revealing that there were crowds of people nearby on the shore—and is shocked to hear nephew and niece agree that this dream scene suggests "diffusion of libido." When Auntie attempts to clarify her position, her niece stops her cold with "*Not* before the children, Aunt."[3]

Light, ironic material such as these two sketches steadily increased Delafield's popularity. And in January of 1927, she hit upon a tactic for increasing her sales which she employed to the end of her career. She created a series.

## General Impressions

A Delafield series requires some explanation. It is not a serial or a story in consecutive installments. Rather, it is made up of short sketches, similar in form and tone, written from a consistent point of view. These appear under a consistent title, with subtitles usually added to give the reader direction and entry into the sketch.

Her idea was a shrewd one. A weekly series kept her name before the reading public more identifiably. And it meant more money. Once an editor accepted a series, her expectancy was whetted along with those of her readers. Delafield found the open-ended nature of series attractive and created at least one a year until her death. Her first series of eight articles, "Imperfect Recollections From the Library of My Youth," drew upon her wide knowledge of children's books and minor Victorian novels to poke gentle fun at venerable works "of moral uplift."

In the fall of 1928, she began a series three times as long, "General Impressions," signed "Wanderer" and marked by clever choice of subject, close description, and witty dialogue. As in "Progress," the point of view is that of a tolerant cynic observing the human comedy, and the form includes a witty general impression supported by specific and dramatic examples. Perfected, this form was one of her journalistic staples. She used it over and over.

Her quickness in detecting incongruity and what she called her "phonographic memory" enabled her to transcribe whole swatches of real talk whenever she placed herself in some remembered scene. Her general impression of the zoo, for example, "that whatever we want to look at is a very long way from where we are now," includes this bit of dialogue:

Spectator (looking at the electric eel): "Did you ever see anything *like that?* It doesn't *seem* like an animal, does it? I mean the way it's

made, and that. How do they ever think *up* the things, is what beats
me."

Her friend (slightly dazed by staring through the glass and water
at a succession of utterly improbable creatures): "I wouldn't like to
have the job of sorting them all out, I know that."[4]

"General Impressions" continued through the summer of
1929, and this series—much of which was published in book
form by Macmillan in 1933—marks another milestone in Delafield's growth as a writer. First, her gift for humor improved
with practice; second, the dictates of sketch writing led toward
the development of her own distinctive form. Journalism demanded a stripped-down, economical style. The comic sketch
required a dramatic technique and an objectivity notably absent
from many of her novels, where thematic seriousness and the
omniscient point of view led her into authorial comment and
discussion. Her general impressions necessitated a scenic method
in which the situation was deftly, briefly set or implied, and
which was then supported by witty dialogue whose pattern revealed the sketch's significance. With the creation of a memorable persona and a recurring cast of characters, Delafield's
distinctive sketch form would come into being. This step lay
just ahead of her.

## End of the First Phase—To 1936

Her success in 1929 was immense. She was the most frequently published writer at *Time and Tide,* aside from regular
columnists. And on 6 December, the Provincial Lady made
her appearance, beginning a new chapter in Delafield's career
which will be retold below. Although the *Diary of a Provincial
Lady* overshadows all of her other work in 1929–30, this was
not her intent.

Her major efforts went into her first play, *To See Ourselves,*
which had a run of six months at the Ambassador's Theater,
and her novel, *Turn Back the Leaves.* And in addition to the
*Diary,* she produced other polished work for *Time and Tide.*
Two kinds of productions received appreciative reader notice:
an ambitious short story that appeared in parts, and literary
parodies titled "The Sincerest Form." One of these exaggerates

the "materialist" details of Arnold Bennett which so offended
Virginia Woolf: "It was 2.5 minutes to four a.m." Another
burlesques devices from her own *Diary.*

By 1930, Delafield was a director of *Time and Tide* and seems
to have had a nearly free hand at the magazine, publishing
whatever she wished. Her output and the variety of that output
are astonishing. In 1931, for instance, she contributed forty-
three pieces to *Time and Tide* alone.

On 10 October, *The Provincial Lady in London* was announced:
"The first of a new series of extracts from the Provincial Lady's
Diary." The sequel was as successful as the original and gave
yet another boost to her reputation. Its English title, *The Provincial Lady Goes Further,* was totally apposite, as Delafield had
by this time acquired her flat in Doughty Street, where she
lived for about half of each year.

While the new *Diary* continued the light satiric vein, Delafield
could play rougher. Her claws, when not sheathed, could cut;
and in "Olympus Spring-cleaned" she shredded Robert Graves
for his *The Real David Copperfield.* Ostensibly rejoicing that *David
Copperfield* "has been rewritten, and made *much* better," she
proceeds to explain Shakespeare's mistakes in *The Merchant of
Venice.* The Bard began well enough, she notes, but then became
muddled and lost his head, allowing "us" to explain his true
intent. But poor Shakespeare's blunders do not daunt "us and
Mr. Graves. We are like that. Free and democratic, and yet at
the same time literary, as you can see by the way we handle
the classics." Much of Shakespeare, "to us," is old-fashioned
after all. "It has no pep. We and Mr. Graves have put the
pep into it."[5]

She began another satire by noting acidly that to parody Michael Arlen one needs only quote him.[6]

In her short stories especially a more serious note intrudes
in the thirties. In the "The Spoilers," Susan, an author Delafield's age, visits a young couple in the country. The day does
not go well; the young couple are frigidly formal and disarm-
ingly honest—not quite human. Talk veers around to the Great
War, and the couple affirm bluntly that they are tired of war
talk. Another war, they believe, is impossible; but even if it
were "we won't take it as seriously as your lot."

The three have walked from the garden into a wood. When

they return, they discover that a brood of pigs has entered their garden, completely destroying it. The young wife drops weeping to her knees "in the middle of the garden, that was now only the spoiled and senseless ruin of what had been."[7]

Tight structure, clean and compact narrative line, objective narrator, and suggestive ambiguity of tone make "The Spoilers" an affective fable. And mark the date—4 November 1933. Delafield hated and feared war. An understanding of her lifelong aversion to it is necessary to appreciate her courage and great sense of duty when war came again, killing her beloved son. Her fable is an early expression of the antiwar sentiment that was to become a dominant note in *Time and Tide* as the decade wore on.

Her series "Let's Remember 1935" gives additional evidence of her patriotic concern for her country. All ten of these pointed criticisms deal with the decay of English social conscience. The operative mechanism is again the contrast between past and present, and these stories make clear her standards for measuring modern lack of principle.

In one, the I-narrator is ridiculed for her old-fashioned ways ("My dear, *all* London is lesbian now, don't you know?").[8] A comparatively harsh tone pervades all of this series, as can be seen in the last, which contains the most direct statement of theme. Here a young housewife angrily refuses to buy from a door-to-door seller. The broomseller persists, saying that he is an ex-serviceman without pension. The housewife explodes, "*Damn* the ex-servicemen. They're nothing but a blasted nuisance," and slams the door in his face. Delafield appended a note to the story stating that "a correspondent" vouches for its truth—"which seems a fitting conclusion—and one requiring no comment to the remembering of 1935—that so signally fails to remember 1914."[9]

Although Delafield continued to contribute each year to *Time and Tide*—her last published work, an acid short story, appeared in it posthumously in 1944—she appeared less frequently after 1935. For she had been invited to write for *Punch,* and most of her comic journalism began to appear there. By 1933, she was a regular and pieces by E. M. D. enlarged her growing readership.

## The Ascendancy of *Punch*

When Delafield was invited in 1933 to contribute regularly to *Punch*, this famous magazine was already the best-known, longest-running comic weekly in the world. A bastion of male humor, *Punch* had opened its pages to women writers—but gingerly. Delafield quickly became the best woman writer at the magazine and satiric humor signed E. M. D. eventually rivaled in popularity that of celebrated veterans like A. P. Herbert.

Her first article, signed "Sportswoman," appeared in December of 1932 and poked fun at a venerable English preoccupation. "The Sporting Spirit" has nothing to say about games, but rather with what family members will say in the New Year (Daddy will say "income tax" a lot).

She began to contribute regularly in the summer, and the *Provincial Lady in America* completed her identification with the magazine with a long run starting in October.

While the new *Provincial Lady* diary appeared consecutively for nineteen weeks, E. M. D. began producing her most famous series, "As Others Hear Us." This began with no fanfare in January of 1934. It continued through 1937, often every week for months at a time, and was only discontinued when the best selections were collected in book form by Macmillan. Its title, like that of her first play, derives from her favorite poem—Robert Burns's "To a Louse"—and the two lines she never tired of quoting encapsulate her philosophy of humor: "O wad some fay the giftie gie us / To see oursel's as ithers see us." With this series, she completely assumed the role of the "fay" or spirit who would strip the mask from social pose and pretension.

The best of the "As Others Hear Us" sketches are little gems. Delafield's quick observation and witty inventiveness assured a variety of character types and situations in which dialogue develops her theme or keynote, as with this "discussion" of modern art by two members of the Bloomsbury avant garde:

"Pattern is what I'm getting at."
"I think that's so absolutely progressive and right."

"Oh, so do I. Nothing matters except pattern."
"Oh, and rhythm."
"Oh, yes, and rhythm. And of course utter starkness."
"Oh, one absolutely must be stark."[10]

This sketch contains some overkill, as well as E. M. D.'s aesthetic bias. It also exemplifies her sensitivity to language, a *Punch* characteristic, which appears in multifarious ways throughout her journalism. In "Vocabulary," "Kinai've that jarrer vasline for crostic, please?" finally translates after some struggle in bridging the generation gap into a daughter's wish to clean her lacrosse stick with vaseline.[11]

These sketches show that Delafield had completed the evolution of a form and stamped it as her own. This form generally features two speakers who reveal the point of the sketch—usually their own egotism or the inanity of the situation—completely through dialogue. They generally share equally in the conversation, although one egotist may dominate it. Varieties within the form range from a whole group of speakers to just one monologist. The enduring comedy of the English character remained the basis for her insights, although her ingenuity in varying subject matter weighed as heavily with her audience as did her technique. Situations are usually typical: a husband and wife or two friends exhibiting age-old behavior in age-old situations. But the situations may be critical, in that a new (comic) decision is reached by one or both speakers. Geneses for these situations, in order of primacy, were: (1) real situations observed, (2) real situations from her own life, and (3) real situations reshaped dramatically through fantasy.

Variety of subject and fine technical control typify the eighty-odd "As Others" sketches, which range from what Suzanne Langer has called free comedy—timeless, universal humor—to Freud's "tendency wit,"—sharp satire. Whether dramatic monologues or comic choruses they are always competent, sometimes brilliant, humor.

## Final Sketch Form

Delafield's last modification of sketch form is undesignated by series title, is characterized by I-narration, and becomes more steadily identifiable through recurring characters, locale, and situations.

As nearly all Delafield's work for *Punch* was signed E. M. D., and as she often drew obviously from her own life for subject matter, the "I" persona became identified with the Provincial Lady—and both with the author herself. Recurring family situations, the use of her family's first names, the familiar point of view—these and similar characteristics encouraged personal application. This tension between fact and fiction—"semi-autobiography" Lady Rhondda called it after Elizabeth's death—helped to establish a warmth of relationship with readers reminiscent of her idols, the great Victorians. The sense that she laughed at herself even as she laughed at others created a bond that was important for her contribution to England's war effort in 1939.

Examples of the undesignated I-form may be found as early as 1935, when more than half of her forty-three signed *Punch* contributions appeared under the "As Others" title. "Enlightenment" for 19 June opens breezily in the first person:

> I like a grateful nature as well as anybody. Moreover, nobody knows better than I do what the Americans have done for this country— crooners, jazz and the English language what it is to-day. O.K. by me, boy.
> So that I was pleased . . . by a rather pretty little dialogue that took place between two ladies in a railway carriage as I travelled from Devonshire to London.

Here a first-person narrator with links to the Provincial Lady seems to introduce a satire on the American tourist. But after the usual pleasantries, during which the English lady, Virginia Woolf's Mrs. Brown, offers to help the American if she can, the tourist asks for an explanation of the English monetary system. Mrs. Brown quickly gets into deep water and fails to provide any enlightenment. The poor American's confusion grows until in desperation she asks, "If it isn't asking too much, I'd be real glad if you could show me one thing, and that's a guinea."

> "I can't," said Mrs. Brown frantically, "it doesn't exist."
> "But in your stores———"

"I know, I know. Things are always marked in guineas and half-
guineas. *But there are no such coins.*"

The narrator steps back in at this point to provide closure—
by stopping the train.

The thing had to stop.
I reached for the communication cord [for use in stopping the train
in an emergency]. . . . [The five pound fine] seemed quite simple
and straightforward.

This anonymous although characterized "I," then, is the chief
feature in Delafield's final sketch form. Another feature is consis-
tency of setting. By 1936 it is clear that E. M. D. has gone
back to the country for her material. A rural locale, felt but
never described, is a constant. Finally, she settled on a consistent
cast of characters, her own *Punch* repertory company, with
whom she peopled this fictional environment.

In addition, short witty articles on books, games, advertising,
and other topics of current interest complemented the dramatic
sketches. War subjects also began to appear, especially civilian
preparations for air raids and invasion. For example, in "Modern
Amenities" (27 April 1938), the home sweet home of the future
features concrete ceilings, small openings onto blank walls instead of windows, fire-fighting apparatus instead of furniture,
and gasmasks instead of pictures on the walls.

It was less than two years away.

## Chapter Five

# The Provincial Lady

Rudyard Kipling's Devil in "The Conundrum of the Workshops" insinuates throughout the poem that clever, popular work probably isn't art. The conundrum has special relevance for Delafield's clever and popular Provincial Lady books—which were not considered artistic, especially by the author, and which are today almost completely unknown.

This chapter addresses the conundrum of an unknown classic. The assumptions that the *Diary* is a classic comedy of manners and the Provincial Lady one of fiction's great characters will be supported by discussions of this work's genesis and development into the natural expression of all that Delafield was as a person and a writer, its formal properties, and its place in her career and in literature. The Provincial Lady books need to be seen in their totality for what they are. As Hemingway so astutely observed, no classic is like any other classic.

## The Provincial Lady Books

In 1930 Delafield's *Diary of a Provincial Lady* became a bestseller in England and America. Its popularity led to sequels which also gained wide popularity. Without realizing how or why, Delafield had created a persona who spoke clearly to women all over the English-speaking world. This persona became a well-known entity in itself and provided a ready role into which Delafield slipped easily throughout the rest of her life.

Although *Straw without Bricks* may constitute a fifth, there are strictly speaking four Provincial Lady books: *Diary of a Provincial Lady* (1930); *The Provincial Lady Goes Further* (U. S. title: *The Provincial Lady in London,* 1932); *The Provincial Lady in America* (1934); and *The Provincial Lady in Wartime* (1939).

The first three of these appeared in one volume in 1935 titled *The Provincial Lady at Home and Abroad* (U. S. title, *The*

*Provincial Lady Omnibus*). In 1947 all four were collected under
the title *The Provincial Lady* (U. S. and Empire title in 1948,
*Provincial Lady Stories*). All four appeared serially ahead of book
publication: *The Provincial Lady in America* in *Punch,* the others
in *Time and Tide.*

No publications records are now available from Harper's,
Delafield's American publisher, but all the diaries remained in
print throughout their author's lifetime. According to records
of her London agent, A. D. Peters, sales of the Provincial Lady
books in all editions exceeded 250,000 copies. The original
*Diary* is the most important of these books, followed closely
by its sequel, and excepting short periods when change of publisher made it unavailable, it has remained steadily in print until
the present. As longevity alone suggests, it is a classic.

## Genesis of a Classic

Although Delafield often said that the *Diary* came into being
by chance, it was actually the result of experiment and experience. The first step toward it can be seen in a sketch from
her *Time and Tide* series which had been running for half a
year. "General Impression: of an English Breakfast," appeared
on 31 May 1929, anticipating the *Diary* by seven months.

This sketch presents a chaotic breakfast in which all of the
family tensions devolve upon the real head of the family, the
wife. Most of these emanate from her husband, significantly
named Robert—the name given later to the Provincial Lady's
husband—who complains about the lack of hot water, missing
articles of clothing, and cold toast. While tending to the children
and inwardly planning her day, the wife commiserates outwardly
with him: " 'Tt . . . Tt . . . Tt . . .' (or whatever the sound
is, that is produced by clicking the tongue against the teeth,
with an expression of deep concern)." Add a characterized I-
narrator and this sketch could stand as a *Diary* entry.

With all the reagents at hand for a successful fictional reaction,
only a catalyst was needed; and Lady Rhondda's request for a
new comic series provided it. "With the Micawber-like conviction that something would turn up," she agreed to write the
new series.[1] Unfortunately, nothing seemed to turn up.

Some weeks later, she attended a *Time and Tide* luncheon

in honor of George Bernard Shaw. It was a funny sort of day as she looked back on it, full of mistaken identities, odd slips of the tongue, and other social incongruities—most of which had the net effect of reducing her self-esteem. On the train back to Devon that evening, she sought to restore her "rather impaired self-esteem" by composing a witty analysis of the luncheon for Lady Rhondda: "And that, actually, was the first installment of the *Diary of a Provincial Lady,* although it was not put onto paper until long afterwards."

Back at Croyle, her title popped into her mind and her conception of the series firmed: she would write, "in the first person singular, a perfectly straightforward account of the many disconcerting facets presented by everyday life to the average woman." She also decided to eschew drama and sentiment, feeling that she was good at neither. The resulting "formula," as she called it, was completely congenial and considerably original. The diary idea, however, was taken from one of her favorite books, George and Weedon Grossmith's *The Diary of a Nobody* (1892). Their nobody, city clerk Charles Pooter, is the historical father of the Provincial Lady, who bears certain resemblances to him.

Delafield was appalled by the mundane nature of her first installment, which appeared as "The Diary of a Provincial Young Lady." An "agonized protest" changed that for the second installment, and after several weeks "One realized, partly from letters written by subscribers, partly from the comments of friends, that readers were enjoying it." Delafield's astonishment grew in proportion to the *Diary's* success, for she could never integrate its popular acclaim with the ease with which she wrote it. The "lamentation from readers," when she brought the *Diary* to a close, surprised her, as did its choice as a Book-of-the-Month selection. Publicity, sales, reviews, and radio and lecture appearances by the author made the Provincial Lady internationally famous. A sequel was called for.

## Sequels

*The Provincial Lady Goes Further* began on 10 October 1931 and ran weekly until 2 April 1932. Book publication the following fall, though not as striking a success as the original *Diary,* was still very gratifying, and again sales in America nearly equaled those in England. The Provincial Lady does indeed go further in this sequel. While country domesticity remains, a London setting takes precedence. Like her creator, the Provincial Lady takes a flat in which to write. The country mouse quality of the persona is maintained, but it is overlaid with new sophistication. Diary entries become cosmopolitan: an artsy Bloomsbury party, club luncheons, dancing parties. The Provincial Lady had arrived, and the obvious element of success in the book enhanced its appeal to women.

Although afraid of type-casting, Delafield bowed to Harper's insistence that the Provincial Lady visit America, and her reports from the colonies began on 4 October 1933 and ran weekly for four months.

The economics of the visit were based upon a series of lectures designed to boost Delafield's popularity and sell books. She thoroughly enjoyed her whirlwind tour, despite two major difficulties. She suffered from deadline pressure, since the Provincial Lady's New World adventures appeared in *Punch* just one week after they occurred. What with constant engagements and traveling, Delafield generally had to write up notes from the day before while breakfasting in bed. The pressure on her London illustrator was even more intense, as he received her copy only a day or two before his drawings were due.

More difficult still was her moral problem. She had been sent to America to write a satiric account of her visit but had "failed to grasp how very difficult it would be to accept kindness and hospitality with one hand, and write a 'funny' book about those who were dispensing them with the other." She liked her subjects, a feeling not normally conducive to satire, and in the end fell back on invented scenes and characters which could have been found in any Western country. Her wit thus inhibited, the result as she realized "was not especially convincing." Nevertheless, both serial and book were well-received and the Provincial Lady's fame grew.

When Delafield contributed her lengthy remarks on these books to D. K. Roberts' *Titles to Fame,* to which this part of the discussion is obviously indebted, she considered this chapter of her career ended. Although editors and readers suggested that the Provincial Lady visit "the South Sea Islands, or the North Pole, or other analagous spots . . . , no one took them seriously, the author least of all."

However, the Provincial Lady was not allowed to pass into history. Within a year of her labeling *The Provincial Lady in America* "the last one," Delafield found herself in Russia for over three months, searching for humor in the Seattle Commune. There was no humor, and it seemed for a time as though there would be no book (she thought at one point of simply writing up her negative impressions and titling them "Harper's Surprise"), but as always she met her deadlines and fulfilled her contracts. *Straw without Bricks* (U. S. title: *I Visit the Soviets*) was both topical and readable.

Its serialization did not, however, work out as planned. *Time and Tide* and *Harper's* pulled the series because of the political protests that poured in after the first installment, a mild satire of Intourist guides. Delafield did not answer her critics in the "Correspondence" column of *Time and Tide* as she usually did when attacked. Her response came instead several weeks later in a comic *Punch* sketch, where she complained humorously that there was no middle ground possible when discussing Russia—one must form two sets of extreme opinions for use with diametrically opposed political views: "which you will refer to either as The Russian Experiment, in a very eager intelligent tone, or as Those Wretched Bolsheviks, in accents of contemptuous horror." Following witty advice on what the visitor returning from Russia can expect, two sample lists of antithetical answers to the same questions are appended.[2]

Her response showed her mettle. The Russian venture was an ordeal for her. As she told an American newsman in 1937, "It's no country for me, and I can't imagine why I ever came to it."[3] Russia was simply too vast and depressing to be worked up into comedy.

It is important to note that the "I" in both magazine and book is clearly identified as E. M. Delafield; but the lure of her famous persona was too strong, and the published book carried the subtitle: "The Provincial Lady Looks at Russia." Thus, author and persona were linked more closely than before. And when she responded wittily in *Punch* to the angry polarization of extreme segments of her readership, she of course used her *Punch* signature, E. M. D. All of her writing stances, even in the novels, were increasingly identified in the last years of her life with the real-life author.

The outbreak of World War II brought home the value to

her country of this identification. Within a month of war's declaration, the Provincial Lady returned to *Time and Tide* to voice the individual's response to the coming struggle with Nazi Germany. Her motives were patriotic, and her strategy aimed at defusing the anxiety of her countrywomen by dealing with surface incongruities of this new social upheaval just as she had always done. She set out on 7 October 1939 to get a wartime job, and kept her readers abreast of her frustrations with this venture until 13 January 1940.

## Formal Properties

Diary entries are arranged chronologically, by date, and begin abruptly with whatever sight, thought, or emotion is uppermost in the Provincial Lady's mind at the moment. Invariably some material fact impels the entry—a situation, movement, speech, or other social activity. This is presented objectively and then ironically commented upon. She finds her subjects in the common stuff of life: defective water taps, dying household plants, balky servants, unresponsive husband, village gossip, and the like—with which she copes outwardly but rages inwardly. These events in her life are presented through loosely connected semiscenes from the point of view of a naive, perplexed onlooker.

There is no attempt at consecutiveness in these diaries. As many as twenty-seven entries may occur for a given month or as few as three. The most important variables seem to have been how exciting Delafield's life was at a given point and how much other work she had in hand. The diaries were uppermost in her mind only when publishers' deadlines were pressing. At one point in *The Provincial Lady Goes Further* a hiatus of five months occurs, and Delafield merely begins again with her 13 April entry by noting: "Immense and inexplicable lapse of time since diary last received my attention. . . ."

Entries also vary widely in length and form—in the *Diary* from two words to over 1,200. The tendency is toward longer entries, several of which are complete dramatic sequences or long editorials. Thus, the *Diary* contains 145 entries, whereas the longest of these books, *The Provincial Lady in Wartime*, contains only forty-five.

Style is elliptical throughout. Pronoun subjects, articles, auxiliary verbs, elements in series are omitted to give a characteristic shorthand, spur-of-the-moment quality. Dialogue is similarly elliptical, almost always indirect, with emphasis given by capitals (e.g., "Robert adopts unsympathetic attitude and says This is Waste of Time and Money").

The Provincial Lady chronicles her hasty reflections on experience through other elliptical devices, whereby the pulse of her personality bears critically upon objective data. After a chilling swim in the ocean this note to herself: "N. B. Never select blue bathing cap again. This may be all right when circulation normal, but otherwise, effect repellent in the extreme."[4] After buying a "vulgar" little phonograph record and deciding how to rationalize her purchase at home, she observes: "Note: Self-knowledge possibly beneficial, but almost always unpleasant to a degree" (*PL,* 147). After the unruly behavior of her children: "Mem.: A mother's influence, if any, almost always disastrous. Children invariably far worse under maternal supervision than any other" (*PL,* 61). After a frustrating social encounter: "Query, mainly rhetorical: why are non-professional women, if married and with children, so frequently referred to as 'leisured?' Answer comes there none."[5] And when formal archness gives way to just plain cattiness, simple parentheses serve. After finally ridding herself of irritating guests—without offering them tea: "Should be sorry to think impulses of hospitality almost entirely dependent on convenience, but cannot altogether escape suspicion that this is so" (*D,* 341).

These formal devices lent themselves easily to parody, even by Delafield herself, but they were useful devices and often copied by imitators. Her standard response to a puzzled questioning of life—"Answer comes there none"—even became in-group slang. While their range is broader than suggested here, these examples show Delafield's typical technique: they are uniformly ironic, usually self-directed even though the implied universal satire on the human condition is often obvious, and they characterize as well as provide comment and tone.

The concrete, immediate humanness of both narrative and comment cannot be overly stressed. People are the center of the Provincial Lady's world, and she worries over their disconcerting foibles as she does over her own. Inanimate objects appear only as settings for human affairs or as extensions of personality. They are included generally, as with any good Dickensian, for their metonymic value.

Delafield's comic characterizations gained additional life from her friend Arthur Watts's illustrations. Like Phiz to Boz, Watts's collaboration was instrumental in the diaries' successes. They discussed their joint venture interminably and drew most of the principal characters from life. Delafield sat for the Provincial Lady. Most surprising, Paul Dashwood posed for Robert, the consistently satirized husband! Watts's penchant for fidelity to fact resulted in charming anecdotes connected with nearly every drawing. Most of his sketches exist, as when he accompanied Delafield to her London hairdresser, where he caught her "at the most unbecoming stage of a permanent wave." As many as three illustrations appear in the weekly serializations, and some twenty are included in each book. These testify both to Watts's demanding craftsmanship and to the fact that his work was indeed a labor of love. "No two people," Delafield said, "were ever more delighted to fall in with one another's views than were Arthur and I over the Provincial Lady."

## The Diaries as Novels

As these books are actually a form of the epistolary novel, they reveal a greater control of form than has been recognized. They yield readily to criticism as novels. Character, plot, theme, setting, tone, point of view—such elements of fiction are handled with an éclat hardly surprising for an author of seventeen novels writing at her best.

Delafield was Dickensianly lavish in creating characters for these diaries, and as all of the fine principal characters plus most of the sharply etched minor types were based on real-life counterparts, the roman à clef quality added another facet of appeal. Aside from her immediate family, for instance, "Dear Rose" is Dr. Margaret Posthuma, "Rose's Vicountess," Lady Rhondda; the "handsome man about town" is Hamish Hamilton; Carolyn Concannon, Lorna Lewis. Close friends appeared by permission; some even sought inclusion. Other "real" people appeared with varying degrees of disguise, in several cases not enough to hide them.

One still-current story concerns a Mrs. Adams, wealthy owner of the large Bradfield estate, which bordered Croyle and for which Paul Dashwood was estate agent. The story goes that at Elizabeth's first introduction to her, this dowager observed coolly, "So you're the wife of my overseer." Elizabeth, better born, was not pleased, and put her prominently into the diaries as the snooty grande dame, Lady Boxe.

Narrative technique is that of the comic strips, where plot tends to be existentially episodic rather than linear, juxtaposition replaces transition, characters enter and exit without preparation and without aging, and there is no closure. Time seems to stand still in the comics; the basic situation of the characters undergoes a variety of permutations but little real change. So it is with the Provincial Lady books.

Yet stasis is only apparent even in the comics; and the Provincial Lady books, static though they may appear, exhibit surprisingly strong plots. The *Diary*, for example, closes with another of the ubiquitous husband / wife cross communications. Returning late from a pompous party at Lady Boxe's,

Robert says, Why don't I get into Bed? I say, Because I am writing my Diary. Robert replies, kindly, but quite definitely, that In his opinion, That is Waste of Time.

I get into bed, and am confronted by Query: Can Robert be right? Can only leave reply to Posterity.

*The Provincial Lady Goes Further* begins with reactions of family and friends to the *Diary*'s success—for example, "rather needless astonishment": "Robert says very little indeed, but sits with copy of book for several evenings, and turns over a page quite often. Eventually he shuts it and says Yes. I ask what he thinks of it, and after a long silence he says that It is Funny—but does not look amused."

The diaries do show plot development; and the main character exhibits considerable growth, especially in the sequels. She solves her financial problems, goes into society, and escapes many of the traps of domesticity. Her children go off to school, she acquires a flat in London, and her *Diary* establishes her as a celebrity in both town and country. Although her anxieties continue, her increased social confidence is manifest, and it grows stronger during her visit to America in the third book.

The main plot, then, takes on the pattern of the success story—
a realistic woman's success. And as readers recognized the close
identification between persona and author, the autobiographical
quality worked to establish a real and continuing sense of kin-
ship.

## Comedy of Manners

American historian Henry Seidel Canby wrote in his review
of *The Provincial Lady Goes Further* that Delafield "is one of
the really skillful novelists of manners in our day."[6] His estimate
is still just. She wrote finished comedies of manners in the novel
form, and all of her comic journalism fits this category. The
diaries, singly and collectively, constitute fine examples of this
comic mode.

Delafield articulates a large cast of stock comic types present
in her society into situations where they either violate social
convention and decorum or are themselves victims. Her reliance
upon dialogue to achieve her comic effects aligns her with the
dramatic masters of the comedy of manners. Finally, her perplexed protagonist in the diaries, a kind of contemporary female
Candide, joins with comparable modern characters to indicate
the evolution of the ingenue hero of satire.

A victim of modern relativity, the Provincial Lady criticizes
from traditional perspectives that conflict with what Delafield
ironically termed "New Age Ideals." Thus, the diaries are all
witty feminist social criticism, and their breadth of comment
is considerable. The *Diary*'s focus on country domesticity, for
instance, balances the Provincial Lady's experience in London
and America. English characters especially represent a wide variety of comic types. Country people tend to be a bit too plodding;
Londoners too slick. Londoners tend to be a bit infra dig in
both manners and morals; country folk too rigid and pharisaical.

The two atmospheres, town and country, are suggested rather
than carefully described. For instance, Delafield restricts the
Provincial Lady primarily to house and immediate neighborhood
in the country, insuring a kind of social claustrophobia. Movement alone summons up the London milieu. A complementary
technique concerns the metonymic value of things—plants, furniture, and the like in the country; things of fashion in town.

The Provincial Lady's self-esteem is tied to successful gardening in one place; to makeup, coiffeur, and dress in the other. In both places she struggles to conform without ever quite succeeding.

Viewed as novels of the comedy of manners type, Delafield's diaries deserve higher critical estimates for technique as well for their historical value. But while they present a faithful social record of their period, they also possess a universality which derives not only from the character of the Provincial Lady but also from their plot-time construction.

For although movement of the main plot is outward and upward as the Provincial Lady grows in stature, the subplots involving the chief recurring characters bump her back to earth. Thus, readers could enjoy her successes but were also called upon to sympathize with her predicaments. These predicaments are timeless and reflect the inevitable rub of society against a sensitive spirit and of that spirit against itself. Her problems with her husband Robert, for example, recur throughout her story; and conflicts with him and within herself because of him cause friction that impedes the forward motion of her life.

So while there is movement and change, there is also timelessness. Entries in the diaries are dated; springtime comes and so does Christmas. But the year is never given, background and certain background characters never change, eventful periods occur but following them "Life resumes its normal course." The hectic yet timeless ebb and flow of a life in flux, still anchored to the common diurnal round, and the Provincial Lady's acceptance of the way things are while at the same time chafing at inevitable constraints give these comedies of manners the universal appeal that perhaps only a historian like Henry Canby would have found worthy of comment.

## The Lady Herself

In December of 1943, the English-speaking world paused for a moment—despite the buzz-bombs, the coming of Christmas, and the Battle of the Bulge—to honor the memory of the Provincial Lady. Obituaries commemorated her as frequently as they did E. M. Delafield, and only a few staid country papers mourned the passing of Mrs. Paul Dashwood. She was sincerely mourned; and in remembrance for the enjoyment she had brought them, a number of readers commemorated her in "little hitherto unpublished anecdotes."

For instance, a Scot recalled visiting Croyle and bringing her tokens of appreciation from a family of fans. These delighted Delafield, and next morning she gave her guest an envelope and said: "Will this do for your friends?" The note inside read: "Profoundly touched by no less than three unsolicited testimonials of extremely handsome description, sent via valued Scotch friend. Should like to meet writers of these, but on second thought perhaps better not, in case they may think better of testimonials. Display these evidences of success to Robert, who says very little."[7] It was so thoughtful, the valued Scotch friend recalled—and so it was, right down to the diary style.

Or this quotation from a Delafield letter: "an unknown and delightful lady approaches me, and says, without preliminary of any kind: how is Robert? which pleases me immensely, and propose to send him a postcard about it tonight."[8]

This last situation was fairly typical of responses Delafield got almost wherever she went; people constantly asked questions about the activities of characters in the Provincial Lady books. And Delafield answered them! For the response cut both ways: if people thought of her as the Provincial Lady, she thought of herself in the same way and was always ready to adopt the role.

It was a perfect role for her. She could draw upon all of the facets of her complex personality and employ her talents to their fullest. Her persona was a reflecting mirror for life as she saw and understood it. At the same time, it freed her to speak out with a sharpness and spontaneity seldom possible for her in her "serious" work. The result is one of the richest characters in comic literature.

She is a keen-eyed observer of people and their mannerisms, which she describes with scrupulous surface realism. The truthfulness of her diaries give them at this point in time a large historical and sociocultural relevance. She judges as well as portrays. Incidents may speak for themselves, but more often yield to her perceptive ironic comment, which while often sharp is always fair. One of her most endearing qualities is that her irony is so often self-directed. She is the one who laughs, but also the one who is laughed at. For example, at a literary gathering, "Am asked what I think of *Harriet Hume* but am unable to say, as I have not read it. Have a depressed feeling that this is going to be another case of *Orlando* about which was perfectly able to talk most intelligently until I read it, and found myself unfortunately unable to understand any of it" (*D, 6*).

Her intelligence precludes sentimentality or self-indulgence. While she struggles to keep her social mask in place and preserve her self-esteem, she readily notes when the mask slips or that esteem is punctured. While she can accept life's incongruities as "the way things are," she also reacts through a surprisingly full range of emotions: irritation, anger, hurt, bitchiness, laughter. Above all laughter. And a tremendous sense of life.

She is unnamed ("call her Mary Smith"), a largely intuitive device that allowed her readers to hear Delafield's voice and that of her symbolic Everywoman simultaneously. She is never described. Her physical appearance, movements, gestures, and other mannerisms are cleverly left to the imagination (although Delafield posed for Watts's illustrations). Her physical surroundings are suggested; they become concrete by assumption or a mere reference. She has effectively no past. Voices from it occasionally reach her, but her life is the minute-by-minute, day-by-day affair of wife, mother, and friend in the turbulence of social flux. Even her speech reaches us elliptically and indirectly. She is sensation mostly, kept in check by a rare and witty intelligence.

Her character develops consistently and fully, however. Patterns of behavior, a core of personality with its characteristic attitudes, and reflections of her in the eyes and manners of others summon up a distinct and vital presence to the mind.

The key to her is the conflict between her inner and outer worlds. The Provincial Lady's desires are modest. She merely wants what every woman wants (and all men): happiness, excitement, love, freedom, and security. More egotistically, she wants to look nice (and to be told so), to be clever and socially smart, to avoid confrontation, and to maintain a calmly superior attitude in the face of life's ups and downs.

What she gets usually is the reverse. Nonhuman things become symbolic of life's refractory nature. They conspire against her, and their dumb, obdurate strength exceeds her own.

Cannot decide whether it is going to be hot or cold, but finally decide Hot, and put on grey-and-white check silk in which I think I look nice, with small black hat. Sky immediately clouds over and everything becomes chilly. Finish packing, weather now definitely cold, and am constrained to unpack blue coat and skirt, with Shetland jumper, and put it on in place of grey-and-white check, which I reluctantly deposit in suitcase, where it will get crushed. Black hat now becomes unsuitable. . . . (*PL,* 28)

Much ado about nothing can be serious business, and such fussing is inevitable when one is on the point of departure for, say, a literary convention in Belgium, as the Provincial Lady is here.

Clothing, hairdo, makeup become metaphors for the insufficient leverage one achieves against the intractable external world, as in the following use of the objective correlative. The Provincial Lady has parted from a good friend in order to dress for an afternoon party, but as usual finds nothing to wear that pleases her: "Query, at this point suggests itself: why does my wardrobe never contain anything except heavy garments suitable for arctic regions, or else extraordinarily flimsy ones suggestive of the tropics? Golden mean apparently non-existent" (*PL,* 177). Disgruntled and feeling dowdy, she rejoins her friend. The friend's dress, of course, "achieves much better results."

The Provincial Lady's obsessive concern with dress is but one of the many metonyms for her conflict with life. Throughout her story, she tries unsuccessfully to find the proper protective coloration that will enable her to successfully blend with her surroundings. And although these difficulties with inanimate things make ready examples, they are as nothing to her problems in effecting satisfactory personal relationships. The world and its people just will not conform to her inner vision of what they should be.

Conflicts between inner and outer occur on a wide spectrum of human relationships, as her life seems to consist entirely of different kinds of adversary relationships: male/female, parent /child, mistress/servant, and the like. Subtler adversaries are found in friends; the subtlest of all are conflicting attributes of the self.

During the course of her peregrinations, the Provincial Lady voices all of Delafield's themes—money, family, personal relations, career. That these are treated humorously did not deceive her women readers, who empathized with the bumps and bruises life gave her and admired her plucky spirit. They fully appreciated that great drama occurs in a few lives only, and that paradoxically these dramas are somehow not as difficult as coping from day to day—as the Provincial Lady does. Her great appeal, then, stemmed not from "serious" drama but from those problems common to us all which seldom find their way into literature.

This appeal was and is not limited to English ladies in country houses. In her preface to the *Diary*'s American edition, Mary Borden praises Delafield's "special neat artistry" and stresses her universality: "The author has an uncanny gift for finding the common denominator of everyday life and of such human relationships as mother and son, husband and wife." Delafield's middle-class Everywoman is still that common denominator.

## The Conundrum: Summary

The story of the Provincial Lady books is inextricably interwoven with Delafield's life and times. We know that diary entries generally record what happened on the date given, and thus that they mirror accurately the social history they cover. We have seen that while her persona is very close to her creator, she is yet a remarkably sophisticated literary creation—and that this creation is objectified through polished technique. Isolable technical features, blended skillfully by the composer, present a structural harmony which though imitated has never in its type been surpassed. For although they are not quite sui generis, the diaries still do not fit present a priori critical systems. They need to be seen as original compositions. Placing them as epistolary novels in the comedy of manners mode constitutes one fruitful critical approach, and they could as profitably be considered as extensions of the diary genre.

Their principal excellence, granting a level of formal competence, consists in their development of a universal character and their openness to life. E. M. Forster believed that "the intensely, stifling human quality of the novel is not to be avoided; the novel is sogged with humanity."[9] And W. J. Harvey observed that "a surplus margin of gratuitous life, a sheer excess of material, a fecundity of detail and invention, a delighted submergence in experience for its own sake—all these are observable in the works of the great novelists."[10] On such grounds the Provincial Lady books richly satisfy. Why then their lack of reputation?

In summary, what the scholar/critic faces in reassessing the diaries is the Conundrum of the Workshop from the Devil's point of view: "It's clever, but is it art?"

Their lost reputations are understandable. Delafield's standing as a writer was never among the highest, and the critical silence that often follows a writer's death has been in her case that much greater. Then, too, cataclysmic changes in our world and its literature wrought by World War II made her domestic fictions seem pale indeed. The idea lingers that her fiction is too polite and cultured to be still relevant. And like Jane Austen, with whom she was compared, Delafield suffers from arguments opposing scale to value. But like Austen, with whom we will compare her below, Delafield's ironic vision is neither negligible nor narrow.

With respect to the diaries, Delafield herself has some responsibility for their lack of reputation. During her life, she generally anticipated the Devil's question and informed all who would listen: No, they are not art.

She never understood the powerful appeal of the Provincial Lady. In part this derived from her conviction that, since the diaries were easy for her, they obviously could not be very good. Although simplicity in the form of clarity was an important principle with her, she never seems to have applied it to the diaries. Then, too, it appeared to her that the form was infinitely repeatable—"there is no particular reason why a Diary should not go on just as long as its writer has strength to hold the pen." That only she could repeat them, as several imitations suggest,[11] eluded her understanding—as did the fact that these books were the evolutionary culmination of formal experimentation. Their successes both amused and irritated her, especially when more serious work never achieved the ranking she wished for it.

Familiarity also bred a certain measure of contempt. As the comic side of her own unconfident nature, her persona could hardly be taken very seriously. In addition, her social class held it bad form to puff one's own work, or indeed give evidence of boastfulness about anything personal. A reticence born of early training plus an acquired shyness and self-effacement would have inhibited Delafield's public enthusiasm for any of her books, let alone the most popular. This aspect of her character was familiar to all who knew her, and it is clear to the discerning reader as well.

Women critics pick up this characteristic more than once. Mary Borden, for example, quotes with approval the Provincial Lady's way of referring to her son, in which she finds a "clue" to the writer's very private emotions: For example, "Robin, whom I refer to in a detached way as 'the boy' so that she shan't think I'm foolish about him." The attitude was completely typical of her.

For the above reasons, Delafield was always willing to denigrate her diaries. In her own words,

> Nothing was as thoroughly baffling as the remark made long afterwards, by a woman to whom I was trying to explain why the Diary was not really my best piece of work: "Ah," she said, with a pitying smile, "I don't suppose you have the least idea of why it's good. You wouldn't understand."
> The more one thinks that over the more unanswerable it becomes.[12]

The lady was right, she did not understand; and the diaries' reputations have suffered because of it. Delafield's attitude toward them too much influenced important literary people of the day, many of whom were her friends; and the idea that they were lightweight, nonserious, and inartistic persists today among her family and friends. Lately, despite continued calls for the *Diary* especially, these books continue a kind of subterranean life, at least partially because they have not received serious critical notice. They are known, if at all, as ladies' books, generic hybrids unamenable to formalist criticism.

But the conundrum is as false as Kipling felt it was. They are all clever, and the *Diary* especially is art of a high order.

## Chapter Six

# The Late Novels: 1930s

Although discussion of Delafield's last two novels belongs to the chapter covering the war years, they are included in this summary survey of her novelistic development.

Looking back from *Late and Soon,* her last novel, the pattern of Delafield's fiction is clear. She struck her main themes in her first novel at age twenty-seven, and in her early novels worked through a number of emotional problems that impeded her mature self-integration. Thus, the pruning out of egotism and false romantic attitudes is central to these books. Unified as they are by theme, structure, and point of view, the early family novels are the most easily and validly grouped together.

The novels of mid-career exhibit wide thematic experimentation with the subject of love. Technical experiment appears also as Delafield broke away from her Victorian models. This period is her most fictional, and prominent concerns of the family novels are muted. She tried to write away from her own life, with the result that these plots tend to be more imaginary—imaginary, not imaginative, for in the best novel of this group, *The Way Things Are,* she returned to the autobiographical bases that ground her best work.

In her last period, family concerns again become prominent, but the problems tend to be those of the adult, not the child. These novels show that she continued to improve with the years. One may credit journalism, playwriting, and film for their increased dramatic quality and firmer organization; maturity and professionalism for their vision and polish. Even critics who did not appreciate her domestic subject matter and feminine perspective began to praise her sophisticated narratives and "readable" style.

## Technical Advance

Delafield used a variety of points of view in these late novels. *Gay Life* opens with an effect tantamount to a long panning camera shot, moves into medium range focus, and then to a series of close-ups. Each character subject to a close-up has his own story, necessary exposition being provided through flashbacks. Multiple selective omniscience, the literary equivalent of this cinematic point of view, serves to disguise the critical narrator, whose laboratorylike analysis of modern nastiness at a French resort seems more objective than it is.

Three novels employ the limited-omniscient point of view more effectively than before. Monica Ingram, the reflector character in *Thank Heaven Fasting,* is a passive formation of upper-class tradition. While the narrator must explain Monica's reactions to certain social stimuli (Monica can hardly be said to think), these explanations are always placed in the past and transmitted through past or past-perfect tenses. The narrator never overbalances her character. Julia, the ten-year-old reflector character in *Nothing Is Safe,* shows equally sophisticated handling. Knowledge of technique and child psychology enabled Delafield to tailor both action and language to the child level. *No One Now Will Know,* written during emotional depression, utilizes three reflector characters, each of them a psychological double for the author.

An equal concern for technique can be seen in structure. Delafield's common practice did not include close revision. She wrote her books as rapidly as she could and sold them. But she had also become by the thirties sensitive to criticism of her novel's weaknesses in organization and thus began to take pains with both the composition and revision of what she thought of as her serious work. Whereas her first nine novels were all built on the same plan, and three are almost identical in size and shape, her last novels vary considerably in length and organization. In her last eight novels, she used traditional chapters only in the two books employing omniscient points of view.

Her later methods of composition can be seen in the notes and correspondence relating to *Gay Life.* She made full preliminary notes for this book: Dickens-like possibilities for character motivation and action, outlines to keep her three plotlines complementary, and checks and rechecks of logistical details.[1] Her manuscript is heavily rewritten. Letters from her friend, novelist A. B. Cox, consist mostly of answers to her questions about plot and criticism of manuscript sections she had sent for his comment.[2]

The results of such efforts were different organizational patterns, more expressive structures. She arranged *Turn Back the Leaves* by sections that deal discontinuously with varying lengths of time. *No One Now Will Know* moves backward in time from present to past in order to displace psychologically the agony of the present.

She increasingly utilized subsections to pattern more carefully. In several late works, small numbered narrative units perform specific functions like presenting scene from more than one perspective, separating reflection from narrative flow, or creating transition. Expressive structure, patterned structural irony, conscious metonomy—such devices are employed with skill and confidence. And while she continued to espouse realistic methods, she increasingly utilized imagery in interior views. Her use of metonym to symbolize the lost past indicates that she was thinking more metaphorically, and these techniques are best discussed as symbolic. One can but suggest her greater artistry in these late works. The effect is really total. She just did everything better as she fully matured.

## Late Themes

Delafield's characteristic themes underwent further modulation in the thirties. Fast cars, boats, and above all people race against a background of social change symbolized by the ubiquitous blaring of radios and auto horns. She continued to satirize the foibles of a superficial society, and by the middle of the decade serious concerns begin to crowd out light irony in her novels.

This seriousness went hand-in-hand with a turning inward, back to biographical bases for her fiction. A sort of rounding off occurred. Having worked fictionally through her early life to achieve self-integration, and having used this integrated self as the satiric norm for her social criticism, she now returned to an analysis of personal concerns from the vantage point of maturity. As she became preoccupied with her own family life, tone darkens. Middle-age, a darkening world situation, rapid social change are partial causes. More critical, the hollowness of life around her mirrored the hollownesses in her own life, occasioning first a sense of transience and then a deep-seated sense of loss that nearly overwhelmed her.

While the sense of loss transmitted in Delafield's last two novels resulted from her deep response to World War II, she suffered from future shock throughout the decade. The poignant *ubi sunt* theme (that universal longing for things past) of *No One Now Will Know* epitomizes a complex emotional response to modern life which can be seen throughout her final period of novel writing.

For this theme, with its age-old question, where are those things of the happy past, first appears in *Turn Back the Leaves,* a turbid novel of Time's destruction of a Catholic family. In *Thank Heaven Fasting* Delafield turned back to another large formative influence, her upper-class training, where family life is similarly destructive. After these two Edwardian novels, *Gay Life* returns to the attack on modern permissiveness.

Mary Morgan's happy family contrasts sharply with the failures in personal and family relationships in the other characters' lives. Like Laura Temple earlier, Mary holds her family together primarily by relinquishing her own emotional needs and romantic aspirations. The same moral imperatives operate in this later novel. Mary is as sexually unawakened and romantically deprived as Laura was, but family duty still ranks higher than personal happiness.

The theme of family threatened by modern dereliction of duty is especially insistent after Delafield's American lecture tour. In *Faster! Faster!,* a career woman's family suffers from maternal neglect caused by her intense career involvement. The two products of divorce in *Nothing Is Safe* suffer likewise from the fast pace of modern life, which breaks up their home and then hurls them from one existential situation to the next. Delafield faced squarely these phenomena resulting from the "New Age Ideals," and in both cases places the blame on adult egotism, by which adults place their happiness before that of their children.

Thus, although the genesis of her last two novels can be located in a specific wartime tragedy, Delafield's preoccupation with forces destructive to family life begins with her first novel of the decade. Simply arranging titles to several of these books suggests the notes of tension, unease, and transience which pervade them. "Gay Life" is anything but gay. The world is too much with us "late and soon," and it moves "faster" and "faster" so that nothing can be counted upon, "nothing is safe."

Delafield's tone was different from others who voiced contemporary anxiety and anger. The "nothing" of *Nothing Is Safe,* like the other nouns in her titles, refers back to family. The traditional concept of family was under attack in the Western world as well as in England. Family was often viewed as old-fashioned, restrictive, and destructive. Delafield's reaction to such views was almost unique among the novelists of her generation.

This family theme is complex and wide-ranging, including subthemes and specific situations too broad for discussion here. But consider one aspect of family life, the father figure. If we except stolid, unimaginative Mervyn Morgan and Copper Winsloe in *Gay Life* and *Faster! Faster!,* there are no effective male parents in these last novels. There are several "modern" fathers, with petty jobs or none, who try to take responsibility for their offsprings' upkeep, but the father figure of the traditional family unit has disappeared; and so, nearly, has the family unit. Male characters are insensitive, selfish, unprincipled. They lack breeding and power, have no control over their lives, and cannot lead. If they come from good family, they tend to be either immature or desperately old-fashioned. They may be cold, dishonest, neurotic, or even degenerate; but except for the one romantic figure in her last novel, they utterly lack nobility of manner or purpose, and they generally lack even common decency. Delafield dealt ambiguously with the male image almost from the beginning, but her last group of men are a strange lot indeed.

And mother figures are not much better.

The underlying causes for the decay of family life are again complex, but one additional element in the pattern may satisfactorily complete it. Rapid change could be accommodated while men believed in an unchanging order beyond the earthly flux. Religion revealed such an order and patterned family life in accordance with it. But Delafield had gradually lost all faith in the efficacy of religion.

## Loss of Religious Faith

The demise of a strong religious tradition underlies Delafield's perception of the cultural decline threatening family life. While characters in the early novels have problems with belief, the background tradition remains strong, as seen in adult figures like Mother Gertrude and Canon Morchard. Religion is scarcely mentioned in the novels of mid-career, however, where its absence forms a symbolic ground tone for the pathology of modern love. But it is only in her late novels that the absence of religion as a moral force is noted as a cause for cultural decline. As symbolic Mummy says in *Nothing is Safe,* "religion just simply doesn't enter into real life nowadays."[3] In Delafield's view, both the strict Catholic tradition of her youth and the gentler Anglican tradition she later supported had foundered on the rocks of modernism. There remained only a Pater-like impression of beauty tinged by nostalgia.

Valentine Arbell in Delafield's last novel summarizes the remains of her religious faith as follows. As *Late and Soon* is itself a last stocktaking and Valentine a thin disguise for Delafield herself, these sentiments may be taken for the author's own.

Valentine liked going to church, but she was aware that her liking was based on sentimental and traditional feeling. It had nothing to do with faith, or even with religion.

The familiar and beautiful words of the Psalms always struck her afresh, the hymns, associated with childhood, gave her a faint nostalgic pleasure. She even found repose in listening to the sound, if not to the actual words of the elderly clergyman's gentle rambling from the pulpit.[4]

"Familiarity," "sentiment," "beauty," "nostalgia," "tradition," "childhood." These words summon up emotional associations which come to Valentine as from another world. That world was Delafield's past. The sounds of the gentle voice of that lost world comfort; the words themselves carry no meaning.

Religion exerted a massive influence on Delafield's life and writing as her biography attests. Her temperament remained a religious one; she never shook off entirely her deeply ingrained early training. At the end of her life, for instance, she hoped to be reunited with Lionel beyond the grave. But she had lost the capacity for orthodox belief.

It seems that her loss of religious faith underlay all the various thematic expressions of loss in her late novels. It is symbolically presented through the three-generations figure so prevalent in these books. *Nothing Is Safe* expresses this paradigm most simply: Grandmamma, a believing Christian, goes regularly to church; her daughter holds the view that religion is totally inapplicable to "real life nowadays"; and her grandchild, Julia, while required to pray by both adults, comes to the realization that praying "doesn't really matter."

The demise of religion as a force in modern life underlay the moral slippage which threatened the family unit. Divorce, sexual license—all the adult egotisms involved in parental failure—these and other thematic elements point up Delafield's concern that modern adult life lay in chaos. "The old traditions" were dying out and nothing solidly supportive was emerging to replace them. With Lionel's death, this sense of transience and loss became so acute that things themselves take on metaphorically a kind of impermanence. In *No One Now Will Know,* empty houses join with images of horse and buggy, frilled petticoats, vanished scenes, and folkways to express her complete sense of loss, and the *ubi sunt* formula repeats incrementally throughout this novel.

With the loss of religious support, Delafield fell back upon the family in order to grasp something permanent, but a shaky impermanence invaded her own family. Lionel's growing maladjustment to life frightened her. Rosamund, her father's daughter, became for a time difficult and critical of her mother. Her friendship with Paul remained intact, but as Valentine puts it in *Late and Soon,* "it isn't enough, just getting on well" (*L,* 81). She began to feel herself a failure as a wife and a parent, and as usual the record is there in her fiction. Claudia Winsloe in *Faster! Faster!,* the overbearing, self-dramatizing career woman, is a harsh self-criticism. With Lionel's death, the worst fears of her fiction became reality.

## Final Vision

Fictional and biographical evidence both support the view that at the end of her life Delafield could not escape the recognition that she had failed in those personal relationships that mattered most. Her need for love was transparent, the strongest desire of her life. It was because of this need that she had joined a convent, and the same need had stopped her from taking final vows. It was a need strikingly apparent to those who knew her well, and it was a need expressed in every novel she wrote.

Her sense of failure in close personal relationships haunted her life, and at the age of fifty-two chances of repairing this loss appeared remote. It must have seemed to her that every value upon which she had based her life was hollow (or to invoke an oft-employed word in the last novels, "unreal"). The passing of tradition and of familiar things large and small forced her to accept life's tragic transience. She had nothing to fall back on; nothing ultimately was safe.

This desperate and yet paradoxically numb emotional state is Lady Valentine Arbell's at the outset of Delafield's last novel, *Late and Soon.* Firmly aligned with aristocratic tradition through title, family, and country house—Valentine's traditional code has walled her off from life, and she sleepwalks through the stultifying round of daily routine. As none of Delafield's psychological doubles is closer to the author than this character conceived in the year of her death, it is difficult not to read the novel as a last fictional testament. Yet Valentine's seemingly irrevocable slide into this deathlike condition is surprisingly, and realistically, reversed. She faces the personal failures of a lifetime, sets aside the crushing load of tradition, finds the true self she has lost, and reaffirms her faith in love and life.

From a biographical perspective, the effect is stunning. By resolving fictionally the thematic conflicts that had recurred throughout her career, Delafield reconciled herself with the way things are in a final, definitive, positive statement.

## Novels of the Thirties

*Turn Back the Leaves* tells of the demise of an English Catholic family, and it so resonantly treats the *ubi sunt* theme that English Catholicism itself becomes the subject. From a psychological perspective, a powerful decomposition process can be observed through the plot: all characters are projections of the author, and their stories rehearse aspects of Delafield's complicated response to her religious background. Her foreword states that she intended no propaganda either for or against the Roman Catholic faith. She wishes only to "hold up a mirror to the psychological and religious environment" of this minority group as it existed "and still exists today."

The glass she holds up mirrors a narrow, repressive, claustrophobic existence destructive to all who live in it. Rigid social rules, close adherence to dogma, and defensive isolation from Protestants form the regimen of Sir Joseph Floyd's family, all but imprisoned on his estate, Yardley. This environment causes extensive damage to the Floyd children who come to realize that their upbringing has made them "abnormal," and that Sir Joseph, the "good Catholic," is the cause of this emotional warping.

When Sir Joseph goes mad after the death of his heir in the Great War, a psychiatrist attributes his insanity to hereditary inbreeding. And this organic symbol of religion's destructiveness receives additional symbolic emphasis through the final decay of his estate, taking that term in its broadest sense.

Delafield closes her story with a brief ironic epilogue set on Armistice Day of 1929. Two insensitive young fox hunters, who care nothing about the history of the Great War or the estate they are hunting on, ignorantly disparage both. The final vignette shows them surveying with disdain the two old women pushing the mad squire in his Bath chair up the overgrown avenue. Lady Floyd and her daughter are indistinguishable from one another to the hunters; and this shift in the point of view relegates the past to existential insignificance. The past is not only dead; it is incomprehensible, mad.

This haunting and brutal allegory covers Delafield's life to the moment of its writing (1890–1929), as she turned back the leaves of her religious past to examine and exorcise its trauma. Temporal discontinuities, images of decay, and shifting focus testify to her difficulties in working up this material. Her symbolic indictment of Catholicism does not square with her objective foreword, and it jostles against the wistful context in which decay imagery often appears. Each of the Floyd children represent a distinct thematic position in her "psychological environment," and one daughter's illegitimacy forms a subplot that poignantly symbolizes the author's own sense of displacement.

In *Challenge to Clarissa* (U. S. title: *House Party*), the wealthy and egotistical title character's challenge is to halt the course of young love. She fails—as does the novel. The latter's firm organization, fine supporting cast, and comic scenes cannot hold up the dead weight of the bland ingenue parts and their pallid romantic conflict.

## Thank Heaven Fasting

This polished, compact novel is a deep and deeply ironic evocation of the atmosphere of a vanished way of life, and it gains great sociocultural authority as the carefully detailed record of one who knew. All of Delafield's considerable talents were brought to bear here: her powers as social analyst; her skill in dramatic comedy; and her great memory for conversations, manners, and gesture.

The novel's title is taken from *As You Like It*. Silvius's idolatry of Phoebe meets with rebuff, whereupon Rosalind steps in behind the pair, chiding Phoebe for refusing Silvius's—indeed any—offer:

> But mistress, know yourself. Down upon your knees,
> And thank heaven, fasting, for a good man's love—
> For I must talk you friendly in your ear,
> Sell when you can, you are not for all markets.
>
> (3.5.57–60)

Delafield's appreciation of the play's ironies influenced her novel, which like the play is essentially trivial in its action. Her own fine structural irony skillfully points up the incongruity between trivial events and the great social weight that invests them. The cynical upper-class social code, that in a tight marriage market—a buyer's market—*any* husband should be gratefully accepted, reveals a societal perversion that Delafield's irony plays with on several levels.

Little Monica Ingram's little story unfolds in three books: "The Eaton Square Tradition," "The Anxious Years," and "The Happy Ending." Her portrayal as a product of upper-class tradition with but one goal in life—a socially acceptable marriage—marks her as a comic mechanism. The all-powerful social machine of which she is a tiny cog regulates her life, and she is an anxious robot, struggling in a Kafka-like way to conform to the machine language she hardly understands.

The plot may be seen as a funnel both in shape and movement.

Book 1, the longest, pits Monica against the Tradition. Its centripetal movement gathers speed and intensity as she moves automatically through the social whirl's mate-selecting process. Her good possibilities for success vanish overnight with a social faux pas trivial in itself, but which nevertheless ruins her reputation. The Anxious Years of book 2 show her socially trapped, funneled into the death-in-life of the old maid. Book 3, the shortest, reverses this movement by announcing the Happy Ending Monica cannot yet see. Dull Mr. Pelham's eleventh-hour proposal in the New Forest is a sophisticated pastoral parody of Monica's earlier vision of the ideal courtship. The serious satire which encouraged the view of mechanical Monica as a social victim relaxes. She regains happiness and self-respect. But although she could not be happier, the novel's structural ironies place her triumph firmly in its thematic and historical contexts. Delafield's oxymoronic ending allows Monica to win everything in one sense, nothing in another.

Monica's carefully controlled characterization is so firmly embedded in her environment that Edwardian upper-class society may be viewed as the novel's major characterization. Environment overshadows protagonist here in much the same way as Hardy's Egdon Heath is the massive determinant in Clym Yeobright's life.

The Eaton Square Tradition, transmitted through adult society, reduces to a finely detailed code of restrictive rules which Monica has been learning since childhood. These explicit and implicit rules leave nothing to chance: "Monica, hold yourself up. Put your shoulders back properly"; "Stand forward, Monica. No one can see you there. Get right in front of me, at once"; "Never put a P.S. It's vulgar."[5] On any given day, "the whole tradition of Monica's world was daily and hourly soaking into her very being, so that it became an ineradicable part of herself, never wholly to be eliminated again from her innermost consciousness" (*TH,* 10). For instance, summoned with the Marlowe sisters to meet a gentleman caller,

On the landing outside the double-doors of the drawing-room, all three paused for a moment and, quite unconsciously, assumed entirely new and artificial expressions before going in.

Monica put her shoulders back, and raised her chin, the echo of countless adjurations to "hold up" returning automatically to her mind, as it always did in the presence of either of her parents. (*TH,* 19)

Or, during a dance at her first ball, "She and her partner did not speak, at first, and Monica had leisure to look at her own reflection in the long glasses on the walls. She saw that she was wearing too serious an expression. Both her mother and the dancing mistress had warned her about this and she immediately assumed an air of fresh, sparkling enjoyment" (*TH,* 45).

Thoroughly imbued with the Tradition, Monica must learn to apply its principles in order to achieve her quest object. Good strategy is of paramount importance:

Never make yourself cheap, darling. It doesn't lead to anything, in the long run, to let a man know that you like him or want him to like you.

Don't talk about being "friends" with a young man, my pet. There's no such thing as a friendship between a girl and a man. Either he wants to marry you, or he doesn't. Nothing else is any good.

A girl who gets herself talked about is done for. Men may dance with her, or flirt with her, but they don't propose. She gets left.

Never have anything to do with a young man who's familiar—asking if he may call you by your Christian name, or write to you, or anything like that. A gentleman doesn't *do* those things to the kind of girl that he respects and might want to marry. (*TH,* 11)

In addition, Monica is warned not to talk too long with a young man (although she must fill any silence with bright chatter) or dance too frequently with the same partner. While she must never miss the slightest opportunity to score a point in the competition for men, she must also cultivate women. Younger women with brothers are of critical importance, but older women of established position must be assiduously courted as well. And no derogatory remarks of any kind must be passed; a reputation for independent critical judgment would be taken as an impertinence and result in lost social opportunities. Finally, in company—when competition is actually in progress—Monica knows to glance frequently at her mother to receive directions by a nod, smile, or other signal to change or continue a present action.

The foregoing can give only a hint of Monica's rule-ridden
environment. The pettiness, externality, and excessive number
of rules point inevitably toward comedy. When Mrs. Ingram
cautions, "My darling, never fall in love with a man who isn't
quite, *quite* . . . ," Monica "ponders very seriously" over this
"perfectly definite and direct piece of advice" (*TH,* 10). But
the comedy turns serious when important rules like those against
flirtation are contravened; and the deeper irony—on which
lesser, lighter ironies like the above float—is that the egregious
Mrs. Ingram is always right. As she notes "simply" when
the goal of Monica's quest can at last be seen: "In a country
where there aren't enough men to go round, girls have got
to take trouble if they want a life of their own" (*TH,* 220).
In such speeches, the novel reaches its deepest levels of irony:
successful adherence to superficial and mechanical "tradition"
meant social life or death to girls of Monica's class and period.

The mass of smoothly textured detail which saturates this
novel assumes a resonance greater than the parts might suggest.
Setting, action, scene, and speech charge mimetic elements with
metaphoric significance. Monica's virginal bedroom with its
childish decor "testifies mutely" to her stunted development.
Indeed, the placement of furniture is metonymic for Tradition
strategy as much as the codified manners which determine social
interaction. Scenes like Monica's first ball are carefully prepared
for and meticulously developed. Delafield's photographic, phonographic memory fixes them definitively, so that the novel as
a whole becomes symbolic for a way of life.

Monica, and to a lesser extent the Marlowe sisters, symbolizes
the traditional training of upper-class Edwardian women. Monica
is the epitome of the Delafield character who can never grasp
reality. She is imaged repeatedly as living the life of a fictional
character, enmeshed in the unreal daydream of the Tradition.
A typical daydream, this one at her first ball, terminates typically
as well:

> "Darling, *wake up!*" hissed her mother.
> People were beginning to arrive.
> Monica put back her shoulders, smiled brightly, and fastened her

white kid gloves preparatory to the exchange of a number of hand-shakes with other white kid gloves. (*TH*, 43)

The typical synecdoche is typically apt.

Delafield manages the limited omniscient point of view per-fectly in this work. The authorial voice stays close to Monica, definitely *in* the world of the characters. She is unobtrusive, yet always ahead of the protagonist creating the irony that struc-tures the novel. The past-tense passive voice makes symbolic Monica's domination by her Tradition a given from the outset: "Much was said in the days of Monica's early youth," "One remembered," "One was safeguarded" (*TH*, 1, 17, 27). Pro-gressive past tenses such as "She was talking almost naturally," "She was living in a dream," join to signal the mechanical, recurring nature of Monica's existence in rendered action as well as authorial comment (*TH*, 60, 83).

Narrative pace results primarily from Delafield's scenic tech-nique, which like her ironic journalistic sketches provides for a preponderance of good dialogue. While she sets up and articu-lates full-dress scenes with extraordinary care, a variety of smaller "semi-scenes"[6] swiftly dramatize recurring patterns and re-sponses in a way that stresses the mechanical, claustrophobic element in the Tradition without slowing the action. This pol-ished little piece moves well.

The immense self-assurance of *Thank Heaven Fasting,* its know-ing quality, stems from the fact that Delafield had lived Monica's life. Encouraged by Lady Rhondda, to whom she dedicated the book, Delafield determined to give a true record of what it had been like for women of her class. The inner emotional record, then, is as accurate as the evocation of the objective social world. The Ingram family faithfully reflects the de la Pas-tures, and Delafield projected the harsher side of her family situation through that of imperious Lady Theodora Marlowe and her two gawky, misfit daughters. Given Delafield's capacity for near-perfect recall and the fact that the two situations tally so closely with available biography, the novel's emotional record becomes powerfully affective.

Biography is put to splendid use in *Thank Heaven Fasting.* The ironies of the marriage market theme redouble when con-

sidered in the light of Delafield's own search for romance. The
novel's technical competence, high finish, and sociocultural
value stamp it like the *Diary of a Provincial Lady* as a book
that merits reconsideration.

## Gay Life

While this novel's themes and some character types appeared
in earlier works, they find fresh expressions here. For her only
non-English setting Delafield chose a resort hotel on the French
Riviera, where her mostly English tourists, all from different
social "worlds," must interact in unfamiliar surroundings.

Its three plots fit solidly into the Delafield canon. All three
deal with the perversion of love by cynical moderns. In addition,
the pathological destructiveness of adult egotism, the unhappy
unparented child, the modern woman's problems in balancing
romantic desire against the call of family duty, and the cynical
materialism of a postwar generation give ample evidence of
the characteristic and related concerns to which Delafield returned throughout her career.

In one plot, an already married pathological liar ruins his
chance for romantic love through his inability to be emotionally
honest. In the second, four cynical sexual adventurers further
mess up their lives and cause the death of a divorcee's young
son. Counterpointed against these, the third plot involves the
sexually unawakened wife, Mary Morgan, who relinquishes romance for the sake of her family. Mary and her family are the
novel's moral center, and her "Relinquishment," the key concept in this thematically rich story, stands in strong contrast to
the actions of the other egotists.

The articulation of Delafield's social criticism reveals a technical reach and sophistication that breaks new ground. *Gay Life*
deals with a disparate social group of varying ages, instead of
using one or more protagonists. It is a novel of perspectives,
the case studies of half-a-dozen characters rather than one. From
the careful interweaving of individual perspectives, one larger
perspective on modern life emerges, shaped by an omniscient
author in a very critical cast of mind.

Delafield managed her point of view—multiple selective omniscience—with genuine virtuosity. A variety of narrative voice

may be found, ranging from objective to highly colored. Although some sympathy for Mary Morgan and young Patrick Romayne is evident, the tone of the novel is hard. The author does not enter the world of her characters, but stays outside and above it—external, distant, judgmental. Delafield's antagonism for her characters allowed for little playfulness and less acceptance.

At the same time, somewhat paradoxically, there is great understanding. The major characters receive full analysis; Delafield's aim obviously was a complete case study of each type. She used action, interaction through dialogue, and subtle authorial comment; but she also employed interior monologue, featuring free indirect speech, to reveal her characters fully, inside and out. The net effect of these complete but clashing perspectives is one of vibrant, frantically desperate life, nicely suited to the material.

Point of view was influenced by the movies, which Delafield thoroughly enjoyed; and her attempt to achieve synchronicity here departs from her usual linear chronological methods. *Gay Life* opens and closes with conscious efforts to emulate film technique. At its outset, a deserted hotel terrace suddenly comes to life. Shouts are heard, heads appear at windows, a bus drives up. This long camera shot establishes setting and context, and then gives way to a medium range shot focusing on the hotel doorway. "In the *opening* doorway [my italics] of the hotel on the top of the white steps, there suddenly appeared—like a conjuring trick—a number of figures." The camera effect then picks up one of these "figures," who begins by interaction to introduce the cast of characters.

The novel's organization—chapters divided into varying numbers of sections—had been employed by her before, but not with the effect that film as narrative model supplied her here. Cuts, dissolves, fade-ins, fade-outs, and close-ups are utilized throughout as narrative focus juxtaposes one group of characters against another, capturing simultaneous pieces of the overall action. And with the conclusion, filmic structure-as-theme fulfills its purpose.

At the close, narrative focus cuts to a panning shot. A French couple is seen arguing; on the terrace below two single women smoke cigarettes and talk, and the point of view sketches in the conflict that will arise between them; below this, an American couple come down the steps in swim suits; and on the main terrace two English women drink tea. As the bus again drives up, the narrator provides the final viewpoint, which could easily be flashed on a movie screen (as in Henry King's conclusion to *The Sun Also Rises*): "Men and women, posturing and chattering, and each one the repository of a secret and complicated history."

*Gay Life,* for all its polish, balances uneasily between novel and filmscript, primarily because of Delafield's penchant for psychological analysis. Concerned with the weight of that analysis, her friend and fellow novelist A. B. Cox cautioned her: "The people should react in action, instead of just thinking all to themselves in corners."[7] His criticism points up the novel's major weakness. Still, *Gay Life* justifies the year and a half Delafield spent on it. She had tried to compete with the best with this book, and although the critics did not reclassify her with the likes of Virginia Woolf, she still received some of her most appreciative reviews.

## Darkening Vision

Delafield's last two novels of the thirties are both exercises in frustration. *Faster! Faster!,* a novel of mid-life crisis, draws heavily on her own life situation, and she lacerated herself through her career-woman alter ego. Claudia Winsloe finds herself trapped by the twin responsibilities of career and family. The harder she works, the faster she moves, the more out of touch with herself and others she becomes.

Claudia represents a new form of egotism; and her characterization seems to have been a new one in English fiction, representing as it does the negative, workaholic side of a career woman's commitment.

Claudia's good qualities ironically lead to her destruction. The plot first sets her up as a modern superwoman—talented, tireless, and selfless—and then attacks her for those very qualities. One after another those close to her discover that her actions stem from her "power complex." She becomes trapped by her power figure role partly from circumstance, partly by her own ego drives. Increasingly isolated, she grows in the novel's terms more and more "unreal"—out of touch with everything, understood by no one. Images of speed support the metaphoric title: all Claudia can do ultimately is to run obsessively faster and faster. "Speed Kills," as traffic signs warn, and Claudia's death in an auto wreck ends her story perfectly.

A victim of Future Shock, Claudia's alienation grows throughout the novel, resulting from noise pollution as well as speed. Traffic noise, the blare of radios, the pressure of people as the megalopolis of London contaminates the country—such phenomena depress Claudia and symbolize her antipathy to modern life.

Her other problems have become all too familiar: morose, out-of-work husband, overly solicitous mother, children who are growing up and away from her. She has acquired family leadership by default, and although she labors manfully to provide a standard of living similar to that she grew up with, the tensions caused by her demanding schedule bring disunity into her family life. She is at once wage earner, wife, and mother. She runs her house, pays for it, commutes to and from work, and tries to deal with the family problems that erupt from this modern life-style.

*Faster! Faster!* anticipates a number of problems that masses of working women would face in the future; and it objectifies the sense of failure felt by its author. The Lewis Carroll epigraph suggests the extent of Delafield's deepening middle-age crisis. In 1936 she saw her life as being in several senses "unreal."

Her daughter recalls asking Delafield, "is that a book all about you?" and her mother answering "Yes." "She was being spiteful about herself," Rosamund recalls, because of something "quite unkind" that a friend had said about her. The criticism triggered a harsh personal reassessment and the projection in fiction of character traits she disliked in herself—and the guilty feelings that resulted. The unrelievedly bleak vision in this novel makes it difficult to imagine much cathartic effect for her from the writing out of these fears and frustrations.

*Nothing Is Safe* continues Delafield's concern for the contemporary family. It chronicles the effect of divorce upon two children during their summer holiday. The breakup of their home makes a chaos of their lives as they are pushed back and forth between parents whose lives have now no place for them.

There are no discussions of marriage and divorce here. Delafield allows structural irony to establish itself merely by watching the children as they are shuttled from one temporary abode to another. What emerges is another picture of adult failure. The effect of this failure on Terry and Julia is one of confusion, strained nerves, loss of resiliance and confidence. Never certain where they are going or when, how they will get there or who will meet them, they lose all sense of balance.

The adults in their lives cannot seem to solve such problems. The children have only each other, but even this companionship will soon be denied them; for the effect upon Terry is to make a nervous child mentally ill. Julia, stronger than her brother, becomes more apprehensive at each new indication of adult carelessness and ineptitude: "What were things coming to, when grown-up people themselves obviously didn't know what to do next, and practically said so, right in front of one?" (*N,* 187).

Although the novel's context is kept purely local, the appellations Mummie and Daddy are writ large in this story: the adult world fails its children utterly. Constantly partying, they have no time for child rearing. They only talk about it. All are facilely conversant with modern psychology; and, as the novel makes clear, psychology has replaced both religion and social tradition.

Although this novel does not seem to be based closely on Delafield's own life, except as imaginative projection, two of its characters came directly from it: her children Lionel and Rosamund were the models from which she drew (in some instances copied) Terry and Julia. Terry looks and acts like Lionel: tall, thin, pale, nervous, hesitant, self-conscious, shy, easily discouraged. He is not dexterous and dislikes the activities normally engaged in by boys his age, preferring instead to read or to play "secret games" with his sister who shields him whenever possible from life. Terry loathes social pressure of any kind and sometimes becomes physically ill (as Lionel was known to have done when criticized or put into new social situations). A mother's boy, men tend not to like him, and even "Daddy said Terry was a neurotic little ass" (*N,* 207).

This resonant little fable deals like its predecessor with newly emerging family problems. Both project their author's darkening vision. While she generally maintained a light ironic tone in her *Punch* articles, the serious side of life intruded more frequently. Her hard-won objectivity had not given her either security or repose. And more serious problems lay ahead for her as her world drifted into war.

## Chapter Seven
# The War Years: Last Novels

World War II overshadows all of Delafield's last work. Although she loathed and feared war, with its coming she gave herself over completely to the service of her country. It was a strenuous effort, requiring all her strength and courage.

It is well to remember the historical context. The seriousness of Britain's problems in rallying the country was not then fully clear. Difficulties in unifying public opinion so that a stand against Nazism could be taken seemed nearly insurmountable, even after Winston Churchill's new government set about reversing Joseph Chamberlain's policy of appeasement. The early part of the war was in reality a war of information, as William Stevenson so startlingly demonstrates in *A Man Called Intrepid.* And the much-ridiculed Ministry of Information's battle to counteract Nazi-inspired propaganda aimed at dividing or breaking British spirit was an uphill one. Delafield, it can now be seen, was one of the soldiers in that battle.

She hated war but was at the same time extremely patriotic. The declaration of war threw her into a flurry of activity in support of Britain's war effort. In less than a year she served on a mission to France, wrote a series of articles praising the French and the Entente Cordiale, tried to bolster morale regularly in *Punch,* worked in a London canteen, wrote *The Provincial Lady in Wartime* for *Time and Tide,* gave patriotic lectures and radio broadcasts, and wrote *People You Love.*

Two of these activities have an intriguing quality about them, suggesting that Delafield played a part in the undercover war during 1940. She offered her services to the Ministry of Information at the war's outbreak and in the spring was sent on an official mission to France. Her friends do not recall the nature of this mission, and the Ministry has no record of it. Later in the year she published *People You Love.* The Ministry has no records of this either, but it evidently provided research assistance, for the book is replete with illustrations, photos, facts, and anecdotes that Delafield could not have obtained alone.

Whether she served in an official capacity or not, she would have found a way to help her country, just as she had in World War I. What should be publicly acknowledged, and unfortunately has not yet been, is that her service—especially early in the war—was important to British morale, that some of it was important to the government, and that this service is still unrecognized.

## People You Love

It seems that the Ministry of Information commissioned this thirty-page booklet as part of its counteroffensive against the powerful Nazi propaganda machine. The support of British women, at whom this piece was aimed, was critical for the war effort—and the British government was not sure of their support. Delafield's choice as the propagandist who could help unite them testifies to her reputation as a feminist spokeswoman.

Her text develops the thesis that "the Nazi is made and not born." She stresses that Nazi brainwashing could be fatal to family life if the Nazis are allowed "to come to" (not conquer) Britain. As "State Property," little boys begin soldiering at age six; little girls become like their mothers part of the brood stock to supply future Storm Troopers for the master race. Women as individuals count as nothing, she asserts, skillfully arguing that women and children would suffer most under Nazi rule.

Her language is simple, her argument straightforward—beamed at the widest possible audience—and she addresses her readers directly: "You little boys," "You mothers." She ends as she began, speaking in her own voice ("I have tried to show you . . ."), using all of her considerable ethical appeal to emphasize the fact that "we have got to win. *Nothing else matters.*" Her peroration shows both her mettle and the patriotic fervor with which she wrote. *People You Love,* an impassioned response to a moment in history, well represents Delafield's furiously energetic efforts on behalf of her imperiled country.

## Wartime Journalism

The imminence of war does not appear in Delafield's *Punch* sketches through August 1939. During these tense months the subject seemed to have been taboo for her. She had written articles and stories condemnatory of war's effects in nearly every previous year, but not now, when it was so close. She turned instead even more to her repertory of country creations in their village, Little-Fiddle-on-the-Green. Comedy of character predominates over satire, and the innocent charm of these last prewar sketches appears much less frequently thereafter.

The coming of the war brought an immediate change in subject matter. Her first articles after the declaration approach propaganda, as her country persona discusses the closeness of bonds existing between England and France.[1] Then in sketches like "Little Fiddle-on-the-Green Stands By," "Keeps Smiling," and "Still Smiling," her villagers slowly gear up for the common cause. Curmudgeonly Miss Littlemug, to whom the government is anathema, decides as a true Briton to nevertheless "give it her *full* support." In the summer, this patriot chuckles bitterly over rationing and in December, still chuckling mirthlessly over her sacrifices, she prepares to cope with evacuees.[2]

Within a month of war's declaration, the Provincial Lady turned out to help the war effort. She was given a huge welcome by *Time and Tide* back "to the pages where she began 10 years ago." *The Provincial Lady in Wartime* began its weekly run on 7 October and continued for over three months, through 13 January 1940. The salutary effect of this timely piece seems to have been great.

One of Delafield's intentions at this time, especially since knowledgeable friends had convinced her that a long ordeal lay ahead for England, was to ignore the war wherever possible and otherwise to keep it in perspective by dealing only with its lighter sides. Thus, in a 20 December 1939 *Punch,* "War and The Author or the Author and War," she urged her readers to avoid newspapers, journals, radios, and return to good books: "A war spent in reading, is a well-spent war." Such discipline, however, was difficult; and as tensions of the Phoney War mounted, war subjects drove all others aside. Before British forces were actually engaged, stuttering governmental efforts to mobilize civilians provided much of the grist for Delafield's satiric mill. The Provincial Lady's battle with bureaucracy forms a running commentary on official confusion, and E. M. D.'s *Punch* persona is equally ironic: "The War has not begun, but

England is in war. There is no shortage of sugar, which is not rationed. But neither is it to eat."[3]

The officialese through which much information and mis-information was relayed to the British public formed a staple subject during these years, as a sample from "Cautious Thinking," illustrates:

> Public health has been standing up well, but we must not on that account assume that we are entitled to feel optimistic about it. There have, it is true, been fewer epidemics than were expected, but until or unless or because or however, we know how many of them *were* expected, and by whom, it will be wise to draw no conclusions of any kind from the undoubted fact that there are not as many as there might have been had there been more. . . .
>
> A temporary increase in the ration of certain nonessential foods may quite possibly, and indeed perhaps probably, be announced in the comparatively near future or, it may be, even a little sooner. Nevertheless the increase, we should do well to remember, should it take place at all, may, and in fact almost probably might, be subject to alteration later on.[4]

A. P. Herbert had for years conducted an unremitting attack in *Punch* on gobbledygook of all kinds, but this four-hundred-word parody compares favorably with his best. The bland passive voice, with its vapid expressions of noninformation, reveals from its opening metaphor and circular, sixty-word second sentence, the stuffy rhetoric of bureaucracy. Niggling qualifications, non sequiturs, contradictions, and hyperbation—that arch suspension of the verb—catch nicely the official mind at work adjusting, trimming, evading.

In one of her many "Talks for the Times," a wartime *Punch* series, a government-sponsored speaker lectures the audience on "how to turn your waste paper into waste paper, so that no paper is being wasted which might be winning the war."[5] Lecturers (Delafield was one herself) went to and fro advising the women of England how to win the war on the home front. Thus, in "Economizing in Little Ways," two of her rustics hike into the village after dark (to conserve petrol), only to hear Miss Seedcage prattle moronically about cutting up dresses to make sofa-throws or brush-and-comb bags. Their journey for knowledge produces none, and as they ruin their clothes trudging home in the dark, no savings result either.[6]

In a 16 October 1940 sketch, "Rivalry," Miss Dodge and "poor Cousin Florence" are found vying bitterly to see who will furnish the homiest bomb shelter. Each time they meet, the new decorating scheme of one of them drives the other to jealously copy the idea: "Miss Dodge took a pencil from her bag, and a fearfully old postage stamp, and made a note on it." Each strips her house to add "that special touch" until Miss Dodge gloats that Cousin Florence can no longer turn around in her shelter. The narrator closes with " 'Cherry Ripe' and 'An al fresco Toilette' looked at least as well [in the shelter] as they had looked on the walls of the dining room."

Delafield mined these and similar veins of humor throughout the Phoney War period. While these sketches range in tone from comedy to satire, and while they deal with a wide variety of home-front subjects, her strategy in all of them was to distract her readers from the horrors of war and to boost their morale.

## The Battle For Britain

Delafield's *Punch* sketches during the first months of the war stay set in her imaginary country village. The additional aspect of her strategy thus included by extension all of rural England, and it also freed her imagination from the turmoil of London. But the Provincial Lady remained in Town, camped out in a makeshift bedroom above the offices of her literary agent. She knew the Blitz first hand and reflected the best spirit of the British during "their finest hour." Londoners' nonchalance, amounting to public disregard, of the worst the Luftwaffe could do, awed the world. Visitors in London during the Blitz (see for instance Quentin Reynold's *London Diary*) were tremendously impressed—as was Hitler.

Delafield's *Punch* piece for Christmas day, 1940, symbolizes her own spirit and the spirit of her country at a critical moment in its history. "Chat in the Basement" consists totally of conversation between two women during an air raid. The main topic of conversation, interrupted often by the noise of bombs, antiaircraft guns, and a trip upstairs to see if one close hit is an incendiary, concerns that rarity, silk stockings:

"Well, my dear, I tried all the usual places and there were simply queues and queues of women, and I saw I hadn't got a chance."

"That was the Cumberland Park gun. Isn't it angelic? I adore it. . . . Go on."

"So do I. . . . Well, it suddenly occurred to me that I could write to Pumbleton Parve, *miles* from anywhere, and see if they'd got any in stock. I don't suppose they sell one pair in six months, as a rule. So I wrote to my old governess who lives there."

"How brilliant! There—do you notice how the house shakes and *still* doesn't fall down? I do call it good."

"So do I. They sound as if they were absolutely looking down the chimney at us, don't they?"

"Yes, exactly. Have some more coffee?"

"Thanks."

"And do go on. (Never mind that, I should think it was yards away.)"

"My dear, she was wonderful. She dashed off, bought up the entire stock—a dozen pair—and sent them to me. Did you ever hear anything like it?"

"Like the stockings, do you mean, or this Blitzkrieg affair."

"Well, both as a matter of fact—but I really meant the stockings. Still the Blitzkrieg is a bit noticeable at the minute, isn't it?"

"Personally, I never will take any notice of it. I'm sure they hate being ignored more than anything. Let's have more coffee, and go on about the stockings. . . ."

The ironic ending of this sketch reveals that the woman with the stockings cannot wear any of them. None fit. And by the time this oft-interrupted conversation concludes, the raid is over.

Although her E. M. D. persona pointed up the comic side of things, Delafield herself often found that pose difficult. To create weekly humor from an inhumane condition she loathed took all her strength of mind and heart. But she accepted this task as her duty. As she told a newspaper correspondent: "My wartime job seems to be to go on trying to be funny, at all costs."[7]

The serious side of this sense of duty emerges from her "Notes by the Way" in *Time and Tide* on 13 July 1940. This popular column was reserved for persons of national or international importance who were invited to express their views on a matter of public concern. Delafield's note further supports the view that her comic talents were consciously and courageously employed in the service of her country. She began, "This is getting beyond a joke," and then asserts that this common English phrase symbolizes her country's spirit: "Because it is precisely at the stage when things are getting 'beyond a joke' that we, as a race, find and make our best and most popular jokes." "In this country, we are not going to be terrorized." However bad it gets, "we" will find something to laugh at. It is our duty.

The supreme test of her philosophy was not long in coming, for on 2 November 1940 the great tragedy of her later life occurred with the death of her son.

Her tremendous sense of loss can be seen in her replies to the condolences of friends immediately afterward. She had been obsessively worried about her sensitive, gentle son's capacity to soldier and wrote, "the thought of his being taken prisoner used to send me nearly mad." She gained some consolation from his being out of a struggle for which he was so unsuited, much from the kind remarks of friends. "Everyone who wrote to me has said the same thing: 'He was always so kind—.' Could one possibly want a better epitaph?"[8]

Her great grief, raw but controlled, was colored by a sense of fate. War had taken her best-loved companion, but it was almost as though she had known it would. And she had experienced the emotions of this tragedy as a writer. Parts of letters at this time are eerily close to the most moving part of her short story, "Not Yet," published in *Time and Tide* on 2 June 1934.

"Can one write a story about what hasn't yet happened," she asks and then sets the scene at the Old Bailey ten to twenty years in the future. A woman is on trial for the murder of her nineteen-year-old son. Before proceeding to sentence, the aged judge asks if she knows of any reason why he should not impose the death sentence. "No," she replies. He then asks, "Have you not something to say—some explanation to give, as to what led you to this . . . unnatural crime?" The woman, overcome with emotion, at last replies:

My lord—it's the war . . . the one we called the Great War. My
father was in it. Both his legs were shot off. He didn't die. Just lived
on, as a cripple. My husband was shell-shocked. He never got really
right again. . . .

I can remember the 1914 war, you see. I know what it did to
them. And when this other war came, and I knew my son would
have to go, I thought what it would do to him. Not only the gas,
and the wounding and the killing, I don't mean. But he'd been taught
to be kind . . . not to hurt things, and destroy them . . . to believe
that hate was wrong. He couldn't have stood the war. . . .

People in court hope faintly that the mother's life may be saved.
Her only defense—"I can remember the last war"—shows
clearly that she is insane. Asterisks set off this irony from the
conclusion.

The old, old judge, with trembling fingers receiving the black cap,
remembers the last war too.
Murder, and insanity . . . murder, and insanity. Those who remember the last war may choose. . . .

The picture of a mother grieving for her dead son is perhaps
the most affective of archetypal situations. Those who knew
Delafield believe, without exception, that Lionel's death brought
about her own. The reaction of this grief-stricken mother is
doubly moving: she missed one week's publication in *Punch*
and then continued on with her duty (see above, her Christmas
Day *Punch*)—being funny at all costs.

## Final Journalism

While Delafield continued somehow to fight off the darkness
with light humor, a harsher note informs much of her journalism
by 1941. For example, in "Digging for Victory," characters
admit to hoarding and then forgetting where they buried their
hoards. Their vicar believes that there is "a great deal more
food in the parish under the ground than above it."[9]

A *Time and Tide* short story, "We're All in it Together," is
more venomous toward a group of well-dressed upper-class characters who complain about the dearth of luxury items, confess
to hoarding soap, and show complete indifference to anything

concerning the war except their own creature comforts. The frame for these petty revelations is provided by a journalist who takes notes on the conversation while waiting for a friend. When her friend arrives, she puts her notes away, thinking sadly: "It's no use: I can't use them. People wouldn't believe it. They'd think I'd made it up." Delafield's moral outrage, judging from the odd letters to the editor later in the month, seems to have sprung from an actual encounter, after which the names of the unpatriotic originals were leaked.[10]

Her unflagging zeal characteristically found outlet in charitable articles and letters. During the summer of 1941, when the Allies seemed to be losing the war all over the world, she wrote "Oliver: an Appeal" for *Time and Tide,* asking all Britons to give to charity "what you can't afford and haven't got." "You can't behave like Bumble and the others," she urged. *"We Will Not Say No!"*[11]

Despite her resolve, a wish-fulfillment theme appears during the last eighteen months of her life. In "Traveller's Tale," for instance, the narrator drives to visit friends, stopping along the way for a steak lunch, for petrol, and for a banana—a Delafield favorite particularly scarce in wartime England. This little day-dream is packed with things commonplace before the war but nearly unheard of in 1943.[12]

While shortages mar the present, threats of straitened circumstances after the war have tarnished the future. An article on "Postwar Planning" defines that phrase as "having less than we do now."[13] "Looking Forward" satirizes once again the proliferation of governmental and journalistic doubletalk: "If it is right that we would begin to look forward to being able to look forward to the beginning of looking forward to the end of the war." This glimpse into the future fails like the others to reassure. The narrator notes postwar controls will be "multiplied, intensified, magnified, and not improbably lead to suicide."[14]

In addition, images of loss and change multiply: silver, plate, furniture, houses, land—these and similar holdings are up for sale, reflecting the economic pinch squeezing England at over one million pounds per day in war costs. Delafield's conviction that the life she had known and had worked so hard to preserve for her family could not survive the war intrudes frequently

into her writing near the end. She repeatedly imaged through
the loss of things her sense that her way of life was passing,
and friends recall her fear that her children would not be able
to keep Croyle.

She accepted the seemingly inevitable with her usual witty
courage. Several satirical suggestions are advanced on the subject "How to go on living in Your Large Country House,"
her dramatic treatment of this theme in "The Capitalists" being
one of the best. In this sketch two country squires discuss their
incredible luck in hanging onto house and hall, even though
they live in back kitchen and dog-kennel respectively. Every
detail, like the bus from the train station which puts the visitor
down "less than a mile from the lodge gates," reverses the
life of prewar days.

The visitor chortles: "We've had the most amazing piece of
luck. There's a Boys' Reformatory in the house at this very
moment," which means that one of his own rooms gets heat.
His friend responds, "But that's simply magnificent! And they
don't mind your staying on yourselves?" The visitor continues
his good-luck story by outlining the privacy he has still: a septic
tank has been installed for the reformatory, and the boys avoid
that part of the garden, which the owners thus "have all to
ourselves."

The irony builds with the responses to each depressing revelation: "Grand," "Splendid," "Capital!" but becomes suddenly
touching as the two old friends plan tea—dinner having been
given up for the duration:

"I know my wife's been killing the fatted calf in your honor. As
a matter of fact, she's got hold of a rabbit."
"I say, I say! Really, I don't feel I ought ———"
"Nonsense, nonsense, old man."
"Well, I've brought a quarter of a pound of tea, and two ozs. of
margarine. . . ."

The guest sighs at the prospect of so much luxury: "Well,
it's grand to be here again, just like old times." His host echoes:
"That's what I say, old chap, quite like old times."[15]

Although in retrospect notes of seriousness and war-weariness
sound clearly through these last sketches, Delafield also wrote

up to her usual level of humor during the last year of her life. She performed her duty ably to the end. Her last published *Punch* sketch is a valediction for her life and her all-but-vanished world. In a "Times Aren't What They Were" for 24 November 1943, she presents the reflections of a Victorian Miss Muffet who grew up in a gentler age: "In those days families had a thing called Family-Life, and we are not concerned here with the terrible damage that it is held by modern thinkers to have wrought, nor yet with the utter incredulity that it meets with from people under twenty-five years of age." Three quarters of the sketch satirizes contemporary manners, the spider finally appearing as one of Little Miss Muffet's earliest memories. Her listeners to these reflections had hoped for "something about Waterloo or Trafalgar" and are disappointed:

> They tried to make the best of it by suggesting that the affair of the spider had affected her whole psychological make-up and probably accounted for all the major errors of her life.
> Miss Muffet, polite to the end, smiled and said that perhaps that was so, but she could not call to mind ever having made *any* major errors in her life.

It was a lovely parting shot. A week after it appeared, she collapsed while lecturing at Oxford and died two days later.

## Summary

Delafield is remembered as a highly skilled professional. Richard Price, who enjoyed her work, has written that her "world of village gentry [represents,] perhaps, one *Punch* tradition at its fullest point of development."[16] This is a generous assessment from a colleague. But it is the "perhaps" and the narrow typecasting so often applied to "lady" writers before the war that might now be dispensed with in Delafield's case in order to suggest for her a larger claim to fame.

The suggestion that her world was comparatively narrow can hardly be a major criticism, since no writer takes all of experience for his province, least of all a humorist. It is unfair perhaps to argue with Price, who valued her achievement; but it is also unfair to allow the idea to continue that Delafield even in her *Punch* journalism confined herself to "village gentry." Translating the hints of narrowness which recurred throughout her career, it would be more accurate to say that Delafield's viewpoint was that of an intelligent, cultured woman—and that certain male reviewers could not at the time sufficiently appreciate it.

Her accomplishment was considerable. Although she is rightly remembered as a writer of cool, accurate, and acidic comic sketches, she also wrote serious articles, affective fables, and other fiction. Reviews, puzzles, letters, parodies, satires, in addition to a variety of sketch forms, point to the fact that she had full command of her journalistic medium. And her total output should be considered: the cumulative effect of years of highly competent work, much of it expressly aimed at service to her country.

In terms of volume of work, originality, technical excellence, and service, Delafield's reputation, on the strength of her journalism alone, deserves to be higher than it is today.

## Last Novels

*No One Now Will Know* and *Late and Soon* are war novels. The genesis of each was the death of Delafield's beloved son. While Lionel is central to both, the sense of deepest loss his death occasioned in his mother was wide as well as deep, for it brought into sharp focus all of the pain of her life and added to that all the anguish caused by the war—such as distress over the passing of her way of life, perhaps of her country. Both novels rank among her best, say in the top four, even with no biographical knowledge. With the aid of biography, both works are very moving. *No One Now Will Know* is a classic piece of Freudian "mourning work," an outpouring of grief elevated by and into art. *Late and Soon* appears to be costume romance; but it represents the completion of mourning, its acceptance, and the spiritual strength to live and love again.

### No One Now Will Know

Delafield's most complex novel departs radically from her usual method. She told this story in reverse, moving backward from 1939 to the two critical events in the novel, which take place sometime in 1900 and 1903, and beyond these events to the beginnings of the Lempriere family in the 1860s. Plot action, necessarily confined to key or representative events, is discontinuous; it is difficult to establish with any surety when most actions take place. In addition to temporal disjunction and blurring, principal characters appear and vanish unexpectedly, the limited knowledge of the three youthful points of view raise important questions but answer almost none, and the adult characters seem in general to suffer from shock.

The plot of this saga is complex aside from the temporal problems its telling creates. Strong-willed Cecilia Odell's marriage to Barbados plantation owner Frederick Lempriere produces three children: Fred, Lucian ("Lucy"), and ungainly Fannie. When Lempriere dies in 1872, his family returns to England, where Cecilia eventually marries an ex-civil servant and moves to his estate, the Grove, in South Wales. This husband dies shortly after the birth of his daughter, Kate, leaving Cecilia alone at the age of fifty, her sons "her only reality."

Gawky Kate is a happy child until her world turns upside down as a result of the whirlwind courtship and marriage of Lucy, her favorite brother, and Rosalie Meredith, her best friend, which leaves her feeling excluded and that she has somehow failed in "personal relationships." Tension at the Grove crescendos when Fred unexpectedly returns and seduces Rosalie.

Two tense, unhappy years follow, eased only by the birth of a daughter, Callie. When Rosalie again becomes pregnant, Lucy believes that Fred has fathered the child. The anguished situation climaxes when Rosalie dies in an accident. The Grove is abandoned: Lucy wanders the world; Cecilia, Fred, and Callie return to Barbados; and Kate joins Fannie's family, the Ballantynes, at Rock Place, their poor Devonshire farm.

Callie grows up (in Barbados, then at Rock Place) surrounded by mystery. Lucy never returns and no one talks about him. When he dies in Nice, France, only Kate is present. After World War I, Callie marries her cousin, Cecil Ballantyne, who has been badly wounded in the war, as has Callie, whose best friend has stolen her fiancé. In 1939, their children Sue and Carol, traveling with wealthy cousins on a last prewar visit to France, arrive at Nice. The young people suddenly remember that their grandfather with the girl's name lies buried there, and they realize that none of them know anything about him.

Like the summary of any thematically dense story, this one

omits the most important aspects of the novel—character, imagery, infrastructure—and *No One Now Will Know* is rich in these elements. But the complexity of this novel is at bottom psychological; and plot information is basic to a discussion of this outstanding feature. All elements of fiction serve the same purpose here: the expression of pain resulting from great loss. The most striking objectification of the complex emotional state from which the novel springs, however, is the fact that all of its characters are psychological doubles.

Delafield had from the beginning, like most novelists, used aspects of her own personality and experience in drawing her characters. Zella de Kervoyou in her first novel is a subjective double for the author as a young girl; and Rosamund and Francie Grantham in her third were created from opposing sides of her personality, a subjective doubling by division. But never before had she used character doubles in such profusion and in so many guises. Never before had they presented such difficulties for interpretation; for without biographical keys, character configurations merely add to the mysterious aura of this complex work.

Fred and Lucy, the most obviously doubled characters, represent opposed archetypes of the male. Fred—dark, massive, indolent, unpredictable—conceals his lack of feeling behind a pleasing exterior and a facile gift for piano playing. His "brutal" sensuality contrasts directly with his brother's sensitivity and capacity for love. Lucy is slighter, fairer, steadier, more active, and has a talent for carpentry and wood-working. Lucy represents the sensitive, competent person Delafield so admired; Fred, the unfeeling, facile entertainer she feared that she was.

Despite their differences, the two are often mistaken for one another. Both are fine horsemen, although significantly neither can control the wild horse representing passion that causes Rosalie's death. Each is the other's only friend. The alter-ego configuration, the light/dark polarity of the love triangle, appears subtly as well as overtly. A servant, for example, announces simply, "Mr. Lempriere"; and when Rosalie expects Lucy, Fred appears. Fred and Lucy symbolize the Don Juan and Tristan archetypes. Neither alone can satisfy Rosalie.

Rosalie and Kate stand respectively for the tragic sides of innocence and experience. Kate is that enduring Delafield char-

acter whose happiness depends upon "human relationships."
Several characters emphasize this fact; here it is Cecilia: "She's
one of the unlucky ones, to whom personal relationships will
always be the first—if not the only—things in life."[17] When
Rosalie falls in love with Lucy, Kate, "who needs to come first
with someone," feels shut out. And when plot dictates a shift
in attention to Rosalie, who must of necessity carry the tragic
theme of experience with its motif of failure in personal relationships to its conclusion, the emotional matrix remains the same:
loss of happiness and hope, self-disgust, agonized submission
to fate.

A more subtle kind of doubling can be discerned through a
recurring situation in the lives of the point-of-view characters
in each part of the novel. Sue, Callie, and Kate are plain and
unsuccessful with men. All three lack effective fathers; the novel's only active mother figure, autocratic Cecilia, raises both
Callie and Kate. Sue's situation is not fully developed, but its
outline represents the culmination of those of her aunt and her
mother (whose likeness at the same age receives comment):
youthful innocence crushed by experience, which is objectified
in part by slights received from a woman friend. Alliteratively
linked Callie and Kate are both actively betrayed, and the motif
of betrayal complements that of tragic loss in the *ubi sunt* theme.
These three characters are essentially one.

Callie further exemplifies the complex psychodynamics supporting the story of this "family so mixed up with one another
in an emotional sort of way" (*NO*, 97), for like other characters
she shifts easily into other double configurations. Of the three
point-of-view characters, she alone gets married—to shy, ineffec-
tual Cecil Ballantyne, shot up in the war. The doubling of these
two hazel-eyed innocents is a marriage in the truest sense: two
characters merging into one. Or the character of Cecilia, who
on the one hand stands for Delafield's own mother and on
the other functions as a subjective character double of the author—for instance, in her being left alone at age fifty (Delafield's
age at Lionel's death) with her sons "her only reality."

Other doublings and character configurations could be
pointed out, but those noted so far point up the extraordinary
psychological relationships that exist among the novel's four
generations of characters. The chain of suffering, springing from

one mysterious cause that links the hazel-eyed Lemprieres (Delafield's beautiful, sad eyes were also hazel), underscores their family identity. Delafield's saga format and narrative complexity obscure her novel's central meaning, but at this point in time cannot disguise the fact that once again she was writing out of intense personal experience, this time of one of the great crises of her life.

Character doubling in fiction functions generally to represent various aspects of the psychological self in conflict. Like dreamwork, "it has the task of portraying all sorts of wishes, fears, thoughts, associations, and so on in the form, for the most part, of 'visual and acoustic memory-traces.' "[18] Doubling further functions as a defense mechanism. It represents the mind's attempt to evade psychic conflict, pain, and confusion; to establish control over chaotic, intensely personal materials through the aesthetic distancing of form; and by so doing to achieve emotional and psychological balance. Psychological fiction deals with basic conflicts which have their origins in childhood, "so that in the psychology of literature we discover that the protagonist is almost invariably a son or a daughter figure. Whatever the point of view used in telling the story, in the formal sense, the psychological point of view is usually that of the child, regardless of the protagonist's chronological age."[19]

Character doubling in *No One Now Will Know* functions in all of these ways. So much of Delafield's love had been bound up for so long in beautiful, maladjusted Lionel that she was simply devastated by his death. "A world without Lionel is not a world I want to live in," she had said.[20] In the long winter of 1940, she had to face that world.

Thus, in her novel she displaces the painful present into the past. The reversed structure, with its movement from present to past, emerges as a defensive tactic that delays encountering and dealing with the tragedy. Dramatic conflict, objectified through the Lucy mystery, can be seen as the formal vehicle that moves inevitably toward the tragedy, uniting the characters in grief and loss and invoking the *ubi sunt* formula: where has he gone? what has happened? why did it happen?

The massive shock of Lionel's death forced open old wounds; and although his loss completely informs the novel it generated, Delafield faced here the pain of a lifetime as well as the immediate tragedy. Grief over her lost son mingled with old grief over her lost father, with psychological scars received from her mother, and with unfulfilled romantic desires and emotional needs. Multiple doubling of characters picks up (and at) all of these old wounds.

Wounded Cecil, whose father "doesn't know what he's done that his eldest son should turn out a milksop," is Lionel; but so is Callie, whose large head and ungainliness project Lionel's maladjustment to life. Kate's life blows up at seventeen, as had Delafield's. The lack of effective, loving parenting, seen repeatedly in her novels, shows once more how deeply scarred she had been by her childhood. All of her accumulated grief and pain reaching back into those lost days—so sad and strange and yet so fresh, which were no more—welled up and overflowed, setting up a reaction that pushed her psychologically back to her youth when she herself had received the scars which never healed. The age of the point-of-view characters in the novel ranges from twelve (Callie) to mid-thirties (Fred and Lucy, in this configuration standing for Elizabeth and her sister Yoe), but the point of view is consistently that of a young person just on the edge of the experience that will ruin his/her life.

The fictional overlapping of her life and Lionel's testifies strongly to their real-life closeness, their almost symbiotic emotional attachment. His death left Elizabeth alone; there was no one with whom she could really share her grief. Worse, she could not talk about his wartime suicide; the question of what he could have been could never be answered. Her old griefs, locked deep within her, could not be shared. And the larger world seemed to be crumbling.

This novel of deepest loss took her back into the past where she clutched at memories of peace and order. The village concert, where Reggie Ballantyne dances and little Cecil avers that his brother hates performing, is such a memory—a happy scene recalling Lionel's dual response to his dancing assignment with a young local belle. Other idyllic memories concern herself, like the social visit in which Callie views the musical snuffbox. Callie does not at this point know of her family's tragedy, but the narrator knows, and lingers lovingly, exquisitely over happier times. Delafield held her grief at a distance in these scenes, mingling memories of safety and happiness from her own child-

hood (the Grove and Aunt Kate owe a good deal to "Aunt
Connie" and her estate in Cornwall) and her children's youthful
happinesses at Croyle (Rock Place).

Such poignant, nostalgic scenes also serve a larger context.
Delafield's son was dead, but other sons would also die. A way
of life, a country, and a culture were at stake as well. The great
sense of loss in this novel, the vivid impression of things sliding,
passing, lost beyond recall, faithfully reflects her deepest fears
during wartime.

Thus, the *ubi sunt* leitmotiv so prevalent in her later work
echoes with greater intensity throughout the novel. Old things—
English things—were passing, dissolving. In this context, her
careful concern for the material and tangible becomes powerfully, structurally apposite. The Grove, symbolic of a lost Eden,
stands silent, empty, and decaying at the end of the family saga.
And in the following, the fictional objectification of removing
her dead son's effects becomes metaphoric for loss of the greatest
dimension.

The blinds were drawn half-down in the big room, and the silk-
and-lace dressing-table bare, as it had been since Rosalie's departure.
The trunk that Kate had packed, was gone.

She knew that the big wardrobe and the long, lavender scented
drawers and shelves were empty, for she had cleared them herself.

Rosalie was not coming back any more.

Kate was waiting.

For what. She had no idea. (*NO*, 295)

*No One Now Will Know* is a powerfully affective novel, unlike
any of her other works. Delafield's agony in composing it can
only be imagined. Prodded by pain she found a form for her
mourning work. This form features structural ingenuity, a fuller
use of imagery than usual in her fiction, which complements
theme and structure, and a complex characterization expressing
deep psychological trauma. Known as a psychological novelist,
this is by far her best work in that mode. Even considering
her Victorian facility for apt titles—and she was known to give
useable titles to her novelist friends—the rightness of this one
seems remarkable. What of the snows of yesteryear? Lost possibilities, present pain, a problematic future? No one now will
know.

## Late and Soon

Delafield took her title from Wordsworth's famous sonnet, "The World is Too Much With Us," and the spirit and movement of her last novel follows that of the poem—from the material, confining world which "wastes our powers" to the free world of natural, spontaneous emotion. Delafield characters had struggled from her first novel onward to repress their desires for a "romantic miracle" and to join instead the world of objective reality. In *Late and Soon,* however, the claims of the "real" world are challenged and, surprisingly in the light of her career, disavowed. A reversal of thematic imperatives, which she had stressed throughout her career, takes place here; and while this reversal is sharp and final, it is also smoothly, believably managed.

The story opens with widowed Lady Valentine Arbell's struggle to preserve her traditional country-house life during wartime. Evacuees from the Blitz live at the back of huge unheated Coombe; but the family still dresses formally for dinner, which an untrained young country girl serves. The menu is monotonous and slender; yet individual menu cards in silver holders announce it daily at table. One of the many outmoded rituals in this Heartbreak House, the incongruity is pointed up by Valentine's younger daughter: "You know," said Jess, "I often think this house is a bit like a madhouse. The way we sit here, and let Ivy wait on us, and all that business of clearing away for dessert when there isn't any dessert—honestly, it's bats, isn't it?" (*L,* 25).

Jess cannot wait to leave home for military service; her older sister, Primrose, who hates her mother and her home, has already left for war work in London; Valentine's brother, Old General LeVallois, slides into senility. Valentine plods wearily through the country gentry's traditional responsibilities: house, village, church, war work.

Scrupulous attention to setting establishes Valentine's environment as metonymic—the objective sterility of her life mirroring the stultification of her spirit. A variety of symbols help to make the point: the entry chime's rusty iron chain which breaks each time someone pulls it, the tennis court which is now a vegetable garden, the Carlylean shawl which is part of

her regular dinner attire (and which becomes "continually en-
tangled in pieces of furniture as she moved"). She is symbolically
trapped in a house that is falling apart, despite her efforts to
hold it together.

The deadly diurnal round Valentine trudges complements
her spiritually suffocating environment. She lives by the noblesse
oblige aristocratic tradition which has formed her, and she cannot take lightly her responsibilities as Lady Arbell, a role which
has an entity all its own. Lady Arbell, for instance, leads the
village women's war efforts, a traditional role for the lady of
the manor, and when she forgets a bandage-rolling meeting,
guilt overwhelms her.

She is a lady in every sense of that term, embodying "the
old traditions": civility, selflessness, duty, and service. "The in-
herited sense of social responsibility" flows strongly through
her, and her self-command carries her through the worst situations. Her "civilized" role enables her to conceal behind an
outwardly imperturbable social manner the deadness within her
and to cope with the pain caused by the failure of her family
life (L, 165, 266, 138, 49).

For a variety of reasons, primarily due to wartime, the traditions of "her world" are called into question, and Valentine
finds it increasingly difficult to define her duty. In this central
conflict, the characters function as rhetorical symbols; they represent positions in the argument. Reggie, the Old General, lives
in the past; his trenchant conservatism and constant reminders
to Valentine to adhere to tradition reveal him to be as antiquated
as the dinosaur. Toothless and arthritic, incapacitated in mind
and body, Reggie symbolizes a dying way of life. His female
counterpart, Valentine's sister-in-law Lady Rockingham, further
exemplifies the worst of hidebound tradition. A typical Delafield
dowager, sneering and imperious, she and her alcoholic, bisex-
ual son testify to its decadence.

Valentine's civilized address to life and people can have nothing in common with such cold, rigid externalities. But neither
can it include the open sensuality and hostility of Primrose,
Jess's casual rejection of her mother's way of life, or the leveling
socialism of young Captain Sedgewick—who congratulates himself on his good fortune at seeing a nearly extinct breed so
close at hand, and who wonders which of them will be "liqui-
dated" when "the Day arrives" (L, 106, 276).

Into this marmoreal environment comes Valentine's romantic love of twenty-eight years earlier (and now Primrose's lover), the Irish artist turned soldier, Colonel Rory Lonergan. The novel's main action takes place at Coombe during the five days Lonergan is billeted there, until he is ordered abroad. He extricates himself from the embraces of Primrose and secures again the love of her mother. He gently, humorously deals with Valentine's fears—and his own—gives her back the confidence and self-esteem she has lost, and takes her away. It is the Sleeping Beauty archetype transmuted realistically into wartime England.

But these lovers cannot escape their problems through romantic flight; they must solve them, and the metamorphosis from Lady Arbell to "Val" requires a completely fresh view of life.

At the personal level, for instance, Lonergan's affair with Primrose, and Primrose's hatred for her mother and all she stands for, paralyzes Val's will. How can she compete with her daughter? What will her world say? Can she "take her own way and still live with herself?" Val poses once again perhaps the key question of all the later novels: Can she place love ahead of duty? Laura Fairchild could not. Mary Morgan likewise chose "Renunciation." Val's problems seem worse, because choosing love in her situations seems to mean replacing her own daughter in an irregular union.

Primrose persuasively presents the case for existential situation ethics. Individuals, she believes, are obliged to snatch what pleasure they can from a contingent wartime situation, knowing that no individual's happiness is important in the face of global grief. She derides "Keltic romance" as a dishonest vestige of outworn traditional moral codes and argues that in transient wartime relationships only simple lust can be honest. She scoffs at Lonergan's romantic desires: "Darling, don't be such a fool. Why in God's name will you always mix up love with this sentimental, romantic bloody nonsense of yours?" (*L,* 64). Love equals sex to Primrose, an idea repugnant to both Val and Lonergan. The truth of the heart's affections is a higher truth for them than sexual fulfillment, but they find their truth difficult to validate in the collision of disparate social worlds and views in the midst of war. They must accept each others' pasts and then forget them. Val must in effect renounce her maternal role in order to join Lonergan; and her problems with Primrose are just one area of social and moral collision for her.

Val's liberation primarily concerns people and their expectations of her, her roles as these affect others. She has symbolically
tried to save the tennis court "for the children," but realizes
that "the children were no more." "Come back [Jess] might
or might not, but the words 'the children' held no meaning
at Coombe, or for its mistress." A more vital reflection, for
the novel's psychological inner meaning, precedes this one:
"Valentine Arbell had never had a son" (*L,* 1, 6, 9). As Lonergan's love restores her self-esteem, she realizes "I've never—
never since I married Humphrey—been my real self" (*L,* 204).
Love makes her a real person who can see through conventional
claims of duty to others to the duty she owes herself.

The claims of love preempt the claims not only of individuals
and of family, but of the world as well. Through the movement
of her heroine, Delafield seems to have brought to a solution
the problem of "World" that had puzzled her for so long. The
world of this novel, variously imaged and dramatized, is composed of smaller discrete worlds. Conflict arises from their collision. Light from the outside world shows Val the narrow
darkness of upper-class tradition. Lonergan is repelled by the
"strange survival of a world" Val inhabits—"an islet upon which
the tide of destruction was swiftly and surely advancing, impelled
now by the forces of war but inevitably due to come, war or
no war" (*L,* 76).

The reality of this world, landlocked from the sea of life,
fades in Val's mind as she realizes in dealing with visiting officers
that people outside Coombe's tradition are as foreign as beings
from another planet: "They would merely exchange the polite
spoken symbols of civilization current between two people belonging to different generations, and, indeed, different worlds."
The reverse, of course, obtains also: Sedgewick, from the same
class as Lonergan, perceives that Lady Valentine "was as completely unreal to him as he probably was to her" (*L,* 98).

The lack of contiguity between the discrete worlds of the
novel represents conceptually the main barrier to the lovers'
union. Not until Lonergan has enabled Val to visualize herself
"in the wider world" can she freely unite her life with his.
When Val completely replaces Lady Arbell, "the romantic miracle, in which she had all her life secretly believed" (*L,* 84),
comes to pass. During the last unhappy night before Lonergan

embarks for an unknown destination, when fears and doubts threaten to separate them forever, a lovely snowfall blankets the Devon countryside: "The outline of every bush and tree was altered and rendered new and unfamiliar" (*L,* 301). Into this new world, the lovers step bravely toward their future.

## "The Romantic Miracle"

*Late and Soon* represents a striking victory of the spirit over life's adversities. Recalling the agony projected through *No One Now Will Know* just two years earlier, this final vision of hope, which closed both her career and her life, testifies again to Delafield's courage and vitality. For her heroine's situation was essentially Delafield's in 1943. Her failure in "personal relationships" seemed complete: Lionel's death spelled the end of her family life, she was ill, and the war weighed heavily upon her.

By identifying Valentine with her creator, this novel's themes can be seen for what they are: Delafield's final resolution of problems that had plagued her throughout her life. The process through which she affirmed love and freedom was like her heroine's: she rejected worldly claims which she felt no longer had any binding force upon her. Delafield's upper-class world, as she recognized repeatedly in her wartime writing, whether serious or comic, was assuredly passing. And the world being carved out by a younger generation, in terms of essential definition, lacked "class." This emerging world would have no place for her and could thus have no claims upon her attention. Duties, large and small, which she had accepted and fulfilled throughout her adult life, could now be discarded. The tradition that had formed her could be safely set aside.

At the heart of Delafield's life, like Valentine's, lay family responsibility, a worrisome concern from which she now freed herself. She no longer needed to make a "home." ("The children were no more." "Valentine Arbell had never had a son.") Not that her heart ever healed from the wound it received when Lionel killed himself. But he was gone. Rosamund remembers painfully the grief-stricken atmosphere which lasted for so long at Croyle. It was so terribly painful that she had to get out of it. At seventeen she joined the WAAF.

Rosamund was her father's daughter; she did not get on well

as a teenager with her mother. There was nothing unnatural in this. Delafield stressed, especially during her last illness, that Rosamund had been a good daughter. But Rosamund is doubled by division in the novel to fill the need for two children. She is the athletic, vital, good-humored Jess; and she is also the sullen, intractable, bitchy Primrose. The vindictiveness of Primrose's portrait, especially the gratuitous new-sexual ethic side of her characterization, suggests the extent of Delafield's hurt feelings.

The hurt resulting from raising a child who becomes critical and independent, and from whom the parent gets little emotional satisfaction or reward, must be universal. Delafield, for instance, wanted her daughter to go to university instead of the WAAF, but Rosamund did not go on to Oxford until after the war. Primrose, then, is a composite that allowed Delafield to take a swipe at her daughter in particular and at callous youth in general. The nastiness of the character gave her creator the psychological distance necessary to help free herself from her deep sense of family responsibility.

Psychological displacement caused Delafield to present Valentine as the survivor of an unhappy marriage and to turn her husband, Paul, into Valentine's brother, Reggie. Paul was still a handsome man, still his wife's companion. But the somewhat ambiguous denigration of the male role, especially of the father figure, which is such a marked feature of her later fiction, continues here. Reggie is ultimately revealed to be a good sort, but he is also insensitive and opinionated, a dead letter, who symbolizes the pressure of male dominance that Delafield could now safely set aside. Unromantic males and marriage receive harsh treatment in her final testament.

Reggie also symbolizes "the old traditions," and although the negative effects of this tradition are themselves symbolized as Carlylean old clothes, Delafield's own position relative to tradition demands some fineness of distinction. Every inch an aristocrat, "civilized" behavior was her *ne plus ultra.* Nothing in her experience ever called this into serious question. But she had always despised playing the gentry; she knew this role too well, and in her final statement on purely external upper-class formalities she firmly dispenses with them.

Alone with the pain of a lifetime, Delafield's situation after

Lionel's death may be imagined. She threw herself into war work, but her illness ended most of that, forcing her to return home to Croyle—to a dull husband, a rather hostile daughter, and to a host of sad memories. She brought Irish novelist Kate O'Brien with her, and at the end of her life instead of pining sadly away she experienced a kind of rebirth.

Kate was seven years younger than Elizabeth. Handsome rather than pretty, Howard Coster's photographs show her to be rather mannish: heavily built with a square face and very short straight hair. Kate sat for Coster three times over a ten-year period and does not appear to have changed at all in appearance from 1931 to 1940.[21] She had broken into print some ten years after Delafield, and her work in the thirties has something in common with her senior's early family novels, dealing as it does with religious and social conflict in a Catholic setting from a woman's point of view.

There may have been some influence or none. Kate's work (especially *Mary Lavelle,* 1936) was explicit in ways Delafield's never was. The important point is that Kate admired Delafield tremendously, professionally as well as personally. She felt that Delafield had never achieved the recognition she deserved; and when her friend's self-esteem had reached its lowest point in twenty-five years, Kate fortunately moved into Croyle to bolster Delafield's sagging sense of self-worth and bring back her zest for living.

Kate's friendship seems to have been responsible for *Late and Soon,* as Delafield reportedly planned to write no more novels after *No One Now Will Know.* That she saw her life as a failure is clear even without using her last two novels as autobiographical gloss. Valentine Arbell's situation brings her own imaginatively to life: "Her sense of having completely failed as a mother was more overwhelming than it had ever been. . . ." Her husband had never given her either happiness or unhappiness. At best their relationship had achieved a little pleasure, at most some discontent." "Valentine had never believed herself to be capable of inspiring passion . . ." (*L,* 160, 14, 91). More weight can be brought to bear on this matter, but Valentine's complete sense of failure—as mother, wife, and woman— before Lonergan's arrival at Coombe parallels Delafield's before Kate entered her life permanently. It requires only a small step to connect the two: Colonel Rory Lonergan stands as a graceful tribute to Kate O'Brien.

Kate's intelligent, good-humored sensitivity fit in well at Croyle in contrast with other of Delafield's woman friends. Rosamund testifies that she and her father liked Kate and that Kate became a part of the family. In her first year at Croyle, she wrote a wartime novel, *The Last of Summer,* one theme of which dealt with French grief over the loss of their homeland and national honor. Perhaps Delafield intended to return the compliment. After her friend's death, Kate wrote a fictional tribute to Delafield's beauty and courage, *That Lady* (1946). As a play in 1949, with Katherine Cornell in the title role, *That Lady* was a success in both England and America.

The lady, Ana de Mendoza, is strikingly beautiful even though she has lost an eye: "Sculptured" is a word Kate used to describe her friend's fine features in her radio memorial of 1945, and she repeated this description in her novel. Ana is a tragic figure, but she is also witty, lively, passionate, and resilient. Her tough courage endures to the end.

Several of Delafield's surviving friends believe that Lady Valentine Arbell catches most of Delafield's essential qualities, for example, the sad shyness so often noted during her last years. But Valentine's affirmation was also Delafield's, and it seems poetically just that the realist who created Val found near the end of her life that she still believed in the "romantic miracle."

*Late and Soon* beautifully affirms this belief in a way that seems too tidy for real life. But after a career spent attempting to prune out romantic attitudes so that an acceptance of the way things are could fully develop, Delafield turned back upon herself in her last novel. Desire for the miracle overpowered claims of the world. Spirit triumphed over matter—as sometimes happens with those who are strong and who believe.

## Chapter Eight

# Perspectives

These final perspectives draw together and emphasize key aspects of Delafield's art touched upon throughout this introductory study. We have thus far commented upon two dozen novels, discussed her classic best-seller, and surveyed more than fifteen years of her best journalism—which still leaves about 20 percent of her work unmentioned. A summary look at this other work, with emphasis upon two outstanding aspects of her art, follows.

## Period Pieces

*Ladies and Gentlemen in Victorian Fiction* ironically enough kept Delafield's name alive in academic circles all the while her fiction was dropping out of print. Its title defines her subject: the "social moralities" of the Victorian upper-middle-class as these were chronicled by a number of minor women writers like Rhoda Broughton, Elizabeth Jewell, and her beloved Charlotte Mary Yonge. These minor Victorians never ceased to give her pleasure. From the beginning to the end of her life, her one hobby of record was reading, and she had literally grown up on the English, American, and French romances which so colored her thinking. She wrote about them, corresponded and traded books with other addicts, and studied them in a scholarly way.

Delafield's interest, as always, resided in people—what the Victorians thought, how they acted, how they dealt with social problems. She found their manners quaintly charming in comparison with the relaxed manners and morals of a postwar world; and she took their minor fiction to be a kind of historical record similar to an album of old photographs. For she assumed that these writers, like herself, tried to present a substantially true record of their times. While this delightful social history grew directly out of a long article Delafield wrote for the *Times* in 1935, its genesis really goes all the way back through the many articles she wrote on Victorians and Victorianism, beginning in the twenties, to her childhood.

Delafield's favorite Victorian, whom she loved even more than Dickens, deserves special mention. She was *the* acknowledged expert on Charlotte Mary Yonge and was primarily responsible for the swell of interest in Yonge's work before World War II. Yonge was the subject for biographical and bibliographical study, lively correspondence, lectures, and numerous articles and citations over the years. Delafield's attitude toward her work may be summed up in one statement: "It is impossible to think of the influences that went into building up the Victorian Age without including Charlotte Mary Yonge."[1] In addition, she empathized tremendously with Yonge's outlook and life, especially her "strange and rigorous upbringing."

Her lifelong involvement with C. M. Yonge would make a fascinating study. Equally fascinating is her Victorian parody, *The Bazalgettes.* Hamish Hamilton published this literary hoax anonymously because Delafield was under contract to Macmillan and Harpers. Word was leaked to London literary and journalistic circles that a prominent writer had written the handsomely bound volume, and a coy "Publisher's Note" attempted to heighten suspense: "This Anonymous novel of the years 1870–76 is something of a literary conundrum and will, we believe cause much discussion. When it came to us the style seemed faintly familiar and we suspected who might have written it. . . ." It would be pleasant to record that the hoax succeeded, but unfortunately no sensation occurred. What remains is a delightful exercise in a minor key.

While Delafield's outrageous romantic plot and her stiffly correct characterizations add to the fun, the chief enjoyment lies in her lighthearted writing. Her sentences radiate the relish she felt for this project, whether through straight comedy, comic allusion, or reduplication of quaint Victorian phrasing: "Is it an effect of the fading light that her face, when she raises it, is ashy-pale?"[2] Her allusiveness constantly delights: little Fanny Bazalgette, dressed up for church, is coyly conscious of her finery, which "finds expression in many nods and becks and wreathed smiles" ( *B,* 87). In the comic subplot, a meretricious Chaucerian poet's first entrance is announced thus: "Blanden is i-cumen in" ( *B,* 142).

Even without knowledge of her great affection for the Victorians and her childlike delight in literary games, the joy Delafield felt in writing this now rare book transmits itself on every page. The elation of little Fanny at the prospect of a fete stands as well for the author's: "O wonderful, wonderful and most wonderful wonderful! And yet again wonderful, and after that out of all whooping!" (*B*, 57).

Another charming period piece, *When Women Love,* contains three novellas on the same theme: a woman cannot be sure of herself in love until her passion has been awakened. The three stories are set, respectively, in Victorian, Edwardian, and contemporary times—complete with period title pages for each. Delafield put a high finish on these fine stories. Period atmosphere is well-maintained through dress, manners, talk, and the conceptualization of "love." Through careful reconstruction of period tone, the noble romanticism of the Victorians gives way to the New Woman and the ironic iconoclasm of the 1890s, and the reader is left with the bleak cynicism of the postwar mood in "We meant to be Happy."

Delafield's lifelong love of the Victorians extended almost indefinitely into print. We should mention her book, *The Brontes,* in passing; and stress that Victorian literature was a very large part of the fabric of her life. Books, articles, speeches, letters, games (some of which she printed), and constant allusions all show her knowledge and love. That she was as effective in dealing with the Edwardians can be seen throughout her work, particularly in her comedy of manners, *Thank Heaven Fasting.* Her period sense was exquisite, and it is to be found as well in her short stories.

## Short Stories and Plays

Delafield's more than one hundred short stories appeared in numerous publications. The best have been reprinted, most of them in three collections: *The Entertainment, Women Are Like That,* and *Love Has No Resurrection*—the best of the three. Even the collected stories vary in quality. At her middle level, the O. Henry formula appears markedly: tight focus, good dialogue and structure, a reversal or epiphany ending in which either the main character or the reader perceives a deeper ironic truth. A handful of her satires of circumstance have real merit, especially because of their perceptive handling of women's concerns.

In her most serious play, *The Glass Wall,* Delafield returned
to her convent days and dealt for the last time with her awful
religious experience. Markedly similar to *Consequences,* this play
takes up again Delafield's main themes: love is necessary for
life; love cannot be satisfied by renouncing the world; women
who live for and through "personal relations" must remain in
the world to find a human object for their loving emotions.

Her title comes from her major metaphor for convent life:
"It's like a glass wall, between the people inside the Convent—
and the ones outside. They can see in and we can see out—
but there's no contact."³ The view Delafield provided through
cloistered convent walls and the action taken by her nun were
controversial enough that the Catholic press rumbled against
the play and the Church blacklisted it.

Delafield wrote other plays, several of which were produced
by BBC radio, but only one adds anything to her reputation.
*To See Ourselves,* her most famous play, appeared in the same
year Robert so perplexed the Provincial Lady and dealt even
more severely with the dull British husband.

The title of this loaded picture of "the average husband and
wife" presents yet another instance of her conceptual debt to
Robert Burns's "To a Louse." The domestic situation of her
average couple, Caroline and Freddie, is devastatingly dull—
because Freddie is devastatingly dull. The conflict concerns Caroline's emotional needs: "Life *oughtn't* to be like this—it isn't
enough"—and Freddie's utter insensitivity to these needs. Caroline tries repeatedly to arouse her near comatose spouse, but
at most succeeds in making him slightly nervous.

> FREDDIE:   I don't know what's the matter with you tonight.
>
> CAROLINE:  Nothing that hasn't been the matter for years, only
>            you've never noticed it. You—you don't take much
>            notice of me anyway, do you Freddie?
>
> FREDDIE:   Why on earth *should* I take any notice of you, dear?
>            You're my wife, aren't you? (act 1)

Freddie simply does not want to be bothered, especially by
anything resembling an emotion. His needs are confined to
the simple, the immediate, and the external: his dinner (punctu-
ally), his bath water (hot), and his privacy (to fall asleep behind

the newspaper). His typical, transparent dullness causes all of the characters to generalize about husbands by basing their observations on him, and a distinction between husbands and men occurs early in the play: men are sensitive; husbands are insensitive. The sensitive male of the subplot reacts against Caroline's sister's attack on male insensitivity with, "I'm afraid you think men are extraordinarily dense!" Jill retorts, "Well, I'm not really talking about men at all—only about husbands" (act 1).

Both of Delafield's plays owe a debt to the Shavian discussion play, and they suffer by comparison. Talky, static, and theme-ridden—both are tied closely to Delafield's life. But while *The Glass Wall* seems too parochial, *To See Ourselves* might well merit production still. Certainly it was a success in its day. It ran for nearly six months at the Ambassador's Theater in London, with young Maurice Evans in the cast, and, produced and staged by Joshua Logan, enjoyed a shorter run in New York. It was printed in Gollancz's *Famous Plays of 1931* and subsequently in *Burns Mantle's Best Plays of 1934–5*. The reason for its success was Freddie.

## Feminism

Like her historical bias, Delafield's feminism cuts across her writing in any mode. The viewpoint is always women's. But while her readers considered her a spokeswoman for women's concerns, and although the Provincial Lady considered herself a "feminist," those who knew Delafield well deny the applicability of that term to her. They point out that she was too well bred for the shrillness and acrimony associated with feminist writing and that she satirized women more frequently than she did men.

It is true that almost no variety of female phoniness escaped Delafield's observation, and that as she never solved the puzzle of maleness her male characters rank of necessity below her fine female figures, but it is also true that she satirized repeatedly the type of Englishman represented by Freddie. Freddie and his frustrated wife Caroline appeared first in her prototypic short story "Appreciation," are next found in *To See Ourselves,* and reappear in sketches down through the years. Freddie is a blood brother of Robert in the Provincial Lady books, Alfred in novels, stories, and sketches, and a number of other male characters in other works. As Delafield observed in introducing a book of cartoons by Pont, "It has been well said—by myself, as it chances—that every Englishman is an average Englishman: it's a national characteristic."[4] There was *one* primary male type, she believed, and nearly every Englishman in his domestic role belonged to it.

George symbolizes the type in Delafield's contribution to *Man, Proud Man,* a "Commentary" on the male by eight women novelists of the *Time and Tide* circle (among them, Rebecca West, G. B. Stern, and Storm Jameson). The title for these eight essays comes from *Measure for Measure:* "but man, proud man, / drest in a little brief authority." Delafield's contribution, "Man and Personal Relations," plays with one of her major themes: man's insensitivity in dealing with his wife and children. She illustrates her theme through ironic remarks on four headings: religion, love, friendship, and parenting. After disposing of George as a dull clod, she adds this proviso: "Because George is not romantic, it does not follow that he is not sentimental." He is. Sports, animals, business, "or anything vital of that sort" generally brings out a rash of sentimentality—which just as generally passes as quickly as it came. But as George never gets in touch with his own emotions or those of others, his personal relations with people remain underdeveloped: "Women sometimes permit themselves to wonder what George's subconscious mind can be like, in view of the number of emotional considerations which he never admits to the light of day. And the simile that suggests itself, is that of a pawnbroker's shop, on the eve of a stocktaking that never actually takes place."[5]

Delafield never took part in any feminist movement, nor did she ever articulate feminist doctrine. She did espouse a woman's point of view dealing with women's concerns and problems in both her serious and humorous writing. In her continuing attack on male insensitivity to women's emotional needs, she was clearly a forerunner of much that was to come. Her feminism, always rooted in her own experience as daughter, woman, wife, mother, and career-woman, makes labeling unsatisfactory and ultimately unnecessary—even though we should no doubt call her a feminist today. Her genius lay in her witty and perceptive analyses of incongruities inherent in women's roles. That she was able to make these concerns typical and give them general significance made her famous with her audience.

Ellen Moers, in her recent history of the "feminine literary tradition," stresses the importance of women writers to social history. She asserts that theorists dealing historically with women's roles must turn to literature for data, "for the depth that only acquaintance with the thought of other times and places can give."[6] Delafield will need to be ranked among the contributors to this tradition.

## Humor

J. B. Priestley observed that the "richest mixture" of humor contains wit, irony, absurdity, a certain closeness to life and affection. Priestley also contended that women have "their own kind of humor" and that while their humor, especially prior to their full emancipation, tended to be narrower than men's, it was also quicker, sharper, less self-indulgent, and more social: "The term *sharp* is important here. Women on the whole have sharper eyes and ears, and when not in the grip of strong emotions have sharper minds, quick to notice pretensions, dubious motives, and all manner of social absurdities. They live closer to life, the actual living tissue of it, than we men do, half lost as we are in doubtful abstractions and vanity, so often lacking in self-knowledge."[7] This eminent humorist's observations catch exactly the quality of E. M. Delafield's achievement, the point to which her hard-won development led.

She was simply a first-rate humorist. While her feminist bias and her firm sense of history and tradition led inevitably toward satire, even her critical comedy was tempered always by human affection and understanding. She is that rarity among humorists: a late-flowering talent that continued to bloom in spite of aging and adversity. She never gave up on people and life. We have seen from examples of her humor in novels, plays, and journalism that her irony ranged across the spectrum from light to dark. At either end of the spectrum lie pure humor and invective respectively. Her gentlest irony is nearly pure humor; invective with her took the form of moral earnestness. With some subjects she could not be indirect. Intermediate forms like parody and mock heroic were well within her grasp, and she shows technical facility all across the spectrum.

Her strengths as a humorist argue most strongly for a place in the history of English literature, and this final perspective aims at giving shape and substance to that argument. As the cacophony of critical terms sometimes drowns out communication on this subject, *humor* will be employed here as the general term, with *comedy* and *irony* as subsets. Comedy's connotations include intellectual criticism; humor connotes warm understanding. Delafield, of course, wrote both; but the general term conveys a truer sense of her development and her typical vision.

Delafield's humorous talents did not develop in any unified way until after her thirtieth year; and their development then, as we have seen, occurred in connection with her work in journalism. Although comic characters and some wit may be found in the early novels, this comic light peers in, as it were, from the periphery. The omniscient narrator is almost never humorous. She is from the first ironic.

David Worcester has typed irony as either "the Ally of Comedy" or "the Ally of Tragedy," and in her early work Delafield's irony veers toward the tragic. Alex Clare in *Consequences* desperately needs to establish a loving personal relationship, but her society has scripted her to hide or falsify her emotions. Increment by increment this ironic pattern weaves Alex's destruction. Worcester calls this form of irony "the satire of frustration" and terms it "cosmic."[8] It forms the negative pole in the spectrum of Delafield's irony.

Movement toward the opposite pole of light irony was difficult for her, as we have seen, although characteristically she made a joke of it: " 'What a number of disadvantages there are in having a reputation for being amusing!' I said, with all that bitterness, gloom and profound pessimism that is so apt to characterize the private life of a humorous writer." An influenza attack, a war scare, "whatever happens people always think that I'm going to be amusing about it."[9]

She fought to gain and then to maintain objectivity throughout her life. The large irony implicit in the title of her first novel is that Zella sees that she does not see. At the end of her situation she wonders if she will ever see "reality." Less than ten years after projecting her own youthful problems ironically through Zella, Delafield's vision had cleared, and her objective eye was sharpening by presenting the British public to themselves in her first journalistic series, "General Impressions." While friction between the objective and the subjective remained the one great constant in all of her writing, and the dialogue of the mind with itself continued to the end, Delafield's irony by the thirties had become inclusive rather than rejective. Her great sense of fun found a vehicle in her journalism, and informed her novels of manners. Light, lively, and discriminating irony began to justify the comparisons of her work with that of Jane Austen, and although her tone would darken, especially in her late novels, she kept her sense of humor alive to the last.

Her considerable reputation as a humorist survived her death, but postwar critics quickly forgot her, although an occasional bibliographic note recalled her "lively yet cool observation," which yielded "its own kind of irony."[10] The long critical silence which ensued was broken only in 1976 when J. B. Priestley recognized her in his *English Humour* as the equal of the best women humorists—even the incomparable Jane Austen. Priestley knew Delafield and knew also of the comparisons of their work. By putting Delafield in the best company, he intended to "set the record straight" by demonstrating the enduring appeal of her humor.

Priestley's classification of Delafield among the best women humorists to have written in English assumes a high level of technical competence, and her full command of humorous techniques is evident by mid-career. The examples given above show that the bulk of her humor yields readily to analysis through existing incongruity theories: humor arising from poorly suited pairings of ideas or situations. She set herself up as that spirit of comic intelligence which showed people as they really looked and sounded, always acknowledging that she drew her material from closely observed life. Like all great comedy, hers is firmly based in reality.

Principal incongruity theorist Henri Bergson viewed comedy as an instrument of social correction and discussed its forms and mechanisms under three headings: situation, language, and character.[11] Delafield's humorous writing presents a plethora of comic situations all based upon incongruity. The disconcerting reply, the puncturing of vanities, those ironic situations that appear over and over in the human comedy—such incongruities form the basis for her humor.

Bergson finds that the most sophisticated comedy is *created* by language rather than merely expressed by it,[12] and once she developed the necessary objectivity, verbal wit became a Delafield trademark. Her quick wit produced many of the "one-liners" recently in vogue, for example her riposte "to parody Michael Arlen one needs only quote him." As examples of verbal incongruity may be given summarily, here are several that suggest her range: at the Hotel Britannia, "all is red plush, irrelevant gilt mouldings, and literary club members" (*PL,* 30); a Belgian asks a pretty English tourist, "What is the English for Autobus," to which she responds, "Charabanc" (*PL,* 35); the Provincial Lady politely urges "our Vicar's wife to come in; she says No, No, it is far too late, really, and comes" (*D,* 97); at an early wartime lecture "on the treatment of shock," a character observes that the only shock she anticipates "is the one we shall all experience when we get something to do."[13] Again, the Provincial Lady becomes involved in a comic romantic crisis during which "a period of fearful stress sets in, and Barbara and Crosbie Carruthers say [tearful good-byes to each other.] They have, says Barbara in tears, parted For Ever, and Life is Over, and will I take the Guides meeting for her tonight— which I agree to do" (*D,* 178). Finally, two English travelers in France discuss (in French) the desirability of speaking French to the French, only to decide (again, in French) that English is the more expressive language ("C'est le plus expressif langage qui est").[14]

These examples show Delafield running the gamut of verbal incongruity. In order, we find simple incongruity, inversion, reversal, transposition in key (shifting the sense of "shock"), strained expectation come to nothing, and cultural incongruity with reversal. A further comic technique involves sensitive handling of the "time-lag" of irony: frustrating the expectations set up by a simple series, for instance, as in the first example above.

Delafield's keen sense for language and her playfulness appear throughout this study in selected quotation. Her humorous techniques invoke every rhetorical possibility: expressive verbs, the mot juste, orthographic devices, and schemes and tropes humorously intended abound in her writing. One trope noted above appears consistently—the Dickensian metonym. In *The Provincial Lady in Wartime,* a Mr. Weatherby is introduced thus: "Mr. W. very tall and cadaverous, and has a beard which makes me think of Agrippa." Thereafter, of course, he is referred to only as Agrippa. At one point in the conversation, the Provincial Lady praises President Roosevelt: "Agrippa seems surprised and I feel would like to contradict me but politeness forbids—and we pass on to cocker spaniels, do not know how or why" (*PW,* 102).

Delafield's typical self-directed irony peeks through here. Somehow the ball always winds up in the Provincial Lady's court, making her feel that she has, however slightly, mishandled the situation. But while her irony is usually critical to some degree, her way of seeing also resulted quite naturally in the purely humorous vision. When the dowager Lady Frobisher invites the Provincial Lady and Robert to dinner to meet the Blamingtons, the Provincial Lady stalls, forcing Lady Frobisher to press her hard over the telephone: "She has promised to produce me . . . and we *must* come. The Blamingtons are wildly excited (have idle and frivolous vision of the Blamingtons standing screaming and dancing at her elbow, waiting to hear the decision)" (*D,* 185).

Exaggeration has long been a basic comic technique, and it fits hand in glove with Bergson's main theoretical insight: a human being invariably becomes comic when there is something mechanical about him.[15] The Blamingtons amuse because we visualize them as puppets responding mechanically like wind-up toys. Bergsonian mechanism may reside in a physical condition, like crossed eyes; it may be an involuntary gesture, like an inevitable scratching of the chin when under stress; or it may reveal a mechanical habit of mind, like Robert's falling asleep each evening behind his newspaper. Whatever its manifestation, it partakes of the absurd and is often given exaggerated expression through comic logic, as the Provincial Lady's mechanical rigidity and her use of comic logic here: "Frightful conviction that I shall miss the train causes me to sit on extreme edge of seat in taxi, leaning well forward, in extraordinarily uncomfortable position that subsequently leads to acute muscular discomfort. However, either this, or other cause unspecified, leads to Victoria being reached with rather more than twenty minutes to spare" (*PL,* 29).

Bergson's last category, the comic in character, is exemplified by the Provincial Lady above and requires little additional discussion. From the unimportant Dickensian walk-on to the Provincial Lady, Delafield's skill in comic characterization can be seen throughout her writing. All three elements—situation, language, and character—require careful orchestration. To support the final argument for recognition of her talent as a humorist, consider this scene from *The Chip and the Block.*

Charles Ellery arrives in Cornwall after a touch of influenza to visit his three children who are recuperating from more serious cases of the disease. His wife, to whom he has also transmitted the flu, is too weak to leave London, although Charles stirs the ire of his children's nurse by announcing that she is "stronger than she looks."

As his cab pulls up at the hotel, Charles crawls from it "with the help of a large walking-stick." "That's a new stick," pipes Victor, his youngest son. Charles expresses his entire satisfaction with his children's health and ignores Nurse Mordaunt's growing irritation over his complacency: "It's wonderful how children throw these things off," he chirrups, "if only we elders could do as much!"

He coughed a little and sighed. "Well, this has pulled me down, but I expect [Cornwall] to do wonders for me. It must. We family breadwinners can't afford to be ill for long, you know."

Father looked at Nurse Mordaunt as he said this, but when she didn't answer he looked at Paul. . . .

Paul, the point of view character, betrays his discomfort, and Charles turns to his daughter, exclaiming over the view and planning a walk with her. "Aha," he shouts, "the open road!": "Father drew himself up—he had been standing with his shoulders bowed, leaning on the stick, since he arrived—and seemed to forget about the stick. He waved it briskly in the air." Delafield allows Charles to rattle on for another hundred words before she interrupts him with the dinner gong from the hotel:

"Come along!" Father shouted gaily, catching Jeannie.
"You're forgetting your stick, Father," said Victor's baby voice.
He pointed to the stick that had fallen unnoticed to the ground.
Father looked at Victor, and Victor looked back at his father. Paul
could not help noticing them.

Paul views the scene but does not understand it. All he feels
is uneasiness.

It was all over—whatever "it" was—in a moment.
Father stooped, slowly and carefully, and picked up the walking-
stick, raising himself with one hand pressed into his back, and groaning
slightly under his breath, began to walk very slowly towards the house,
once more leaning heavily on the stick. (*CB,* chap. 1)

The discriminating irony in this scene recalls that of Jane
Austen. Phoney Charles is carefully set up. His *large* stick, his
exclamatory speech, his comic absent-mindedness are lovingly
built up. The clues leading to the revelation of his pose are
unforced. Nurse Mordaunt's silence and Charles's waving his
stick are quite natural. A nice balance and sense of timing are
evident, too. Little Victor, whose eyes are only for the walking-
stick, speaks twice, each time his father moves; and while Paul's
point of view points up the satiric hit, the understated closure
of the scene allows it to speak for itself.

## Summary

Priestley's implicit comparison of E. M. Delafield with Jane
Austen is neither wishful nor willful. Both women, for example,
were omnivorous readers of novels. Both were ferociously verbal, essentially feminine, similar in temperament and outlook.
While the two writers are comparable in many ways, the reason
for comparing them is not to attempt to equate them. It is,
rather, to demonstrate the validity of E. M. Delafield's creden-
tials as a humorist.

Delafield created memorable characters whose dramatic conflicts with social manners and mores retain their appeal: "Her
way led through the world of men and women in their personal
relationships." She created art "from the dreary intercourse of
daily life," exploring to the full "the possibilities of domestic
humor." Her work was "self-limiting," exhibiting a restricted

focus, and furthermore marked by clearness and lucidity: she is among "the least recondite" of authors. Yet her work has depth beyond what its mimetic surface suggests, primarily because of her controlled and discriminating irony. She utilizes "humor as a way of criticizing characters and their society; and irony as a means of moral evaluation."[16]

These few critical comments summarize the main headings of modern Jane Austen criticism. They describe Delafield at her best as well: small fictional world, overwhelming concern with personal relationships, dramatic method, witty ironic tone, lucid, readable style. The bases for negative criticism, and in Delafield's case neglect, appear here, too: simplicity, narrowness, feminine subjects and point of view. In the old scale versus stature argument, women writers have in the past often been found wanting: their domestic visions omit too much of life. In the case of Austen, Henry James once wondered if a novel of the future might not begin where Austen's usually end.

An important note here: comparisons with Austen are flattering to Delafield, whether they deal with Austen's strengths or her "feminine weaknesses." But historical differences set a limit to them. Whereas Austen's fictional world is informed by eighteenth-century rationalism, Delafield's fragmented world reflects the chaos of the twentieth century. Her "small square two inches of ivory" was constantly smeared by contaminating outside pressures. That this furiously committed, self-divided woman won a reputation for cool, dry wit testifies again to her strength of character and skill as a writer.

Although James's demurrals find its echoes in Austen criticism, such critical positions have now largely been abandoned as sexist and tunnel-visioned. At least feminist criticism now recognizes a female literary tradition, which while different is not inferior to that of men. James's formalistic aesthetic imperatives, in other words, are not the best measure of Austen's moral comedy.

This is essentially Malcolm Bradbury's position as he argues against a too rigidly aesthetic criticism of Austen's work, using James as his focal point. James presumed that Austen observed rather than composed, that her mimetic method dealt so closely with real life that it could not attain to high art. But all novels which interest the reader, Bradbury feels, bring aesthetic order to raw life. It is only a preoccupation with "symbolist and aesthetic notions of fictional creation" that cause us to forget this fact: "There are novels which appeal to the socially normative or comprehensible more than others: novels of manners rather than romances or existential novels or works of high aesthetic composition."[17]

Such an approach to Delafield's work would help to rescue her reputation from the obscurity into which it has fallen.

Bradbury's argument for a reasonable pluralistic criticism tailored to the specific *kind* of novel under discussion has been made also by Norman Friedman, Robert Langbaum, and others. Considered in the light of a now-recognized feminine literary tradition, in which for example domestic subjects from a strictly feminine perspective are to be appreciated for what they are, a pluralist approach would allow for a reassessment of Delafield's achievement in all its facets. And it could stimulate criticism of her work in areas important to the history of English literature: feminist, humorist, journalist, sociocultural critic, and psychological novelist.

Her accomplishment as writer and speaker reveals both breadth and depth. While she spent her talent lavishly rather than concentrating it, specific works of high quality should now be isolated for study from the mass of her prolific output. Although she cannot be ranked as the equal of a towering figure like Jane Austen, as we have seen she can stand comparison with her. Like Browning's Andrea del Sarto, her "forthright artists's hand" produced a body of notable work, especially in humor. And as Virginia Woolf showed in "Women and Fiction," the extraordinary woman artist's achievement assumes classic proportions only in the context of the art of her peers—women who stuck close to the surface reality of the life most women of their time lived. Such writers provide the cultural glue that fastens together our social and artistic history. Without them, cultural continuities cannot be properly understood or appreciated.

E. M. Delafield, distinguished woman of letters, deserves a place, however small, in the Great Tradition.

# Notes and References

*Preface*

    1. Ellen Moers, *Literary Women* (London: Women's Press, 1980), xiii.

*Chapter One*

    1. Taped interview with Rosamund Dashwood, Galiano Island, summer 1977. This first biographical note on E. M. Delafield would have been impossible without her daughter's help, and she is the source of information not ascribed to other sources.

    2. "Brides of Heaven," Delafield Collection 3–11, Library, University of British Columbia. Material quoted or unquoted pertaining to Delafield's convent life comes from this manuscript unless otherwise indicated.

    3. Both her novel *Consequences* and play *The Glass Wall* present a different version. In these, the young nun renounces her vows because of her love for the mother superior who leaves for South America.

    4. The narrator describing Alex Clare in *Consequences* (London, 1919), 285; hereafter cited in the text as *C.*

    5. Interview with Mrs. Marjorie Watts, London, 1979. Marjorie, Elizabeth's friend, is the daughter of P.E.N. Club founder, C. A. Dawson-Scott. She acted as club secretary during the twenties when John Galsworthy was president and most important European writers were members. She married Arthur Watts—artist, *Punch* cartoonist, and illustrator of the Provincial Lady books—also Elizabeth's friend.

    6. *Punch,* 9 May 1934.

    7. "E. M. Delafield As I Knew Her," BBC Radio, 19 March 1941.

    8. Of those who knew Mrs. Dashwood, Percy Lane, Henry Frost, Richard and Anne Milton, and Leslie Leatt are referred to here.

    9. Interview with Hamish Hamilton, summer 1977; interview with J. B. Priestley, winter 1980.

    10. *Dundee Telegraph,* in Delafield Collection, 3–8.

    11. Delafield to Hamish Hamilton, 26 November 1940.

*Chapter Two*

1. *The War Workers* (London, 1918), 272; hereafter cited in the text as *WW*.
2. *The Pelicans* (London, 1918), 334; hereafter cited in the text as *P.*
3. Lionel Stevenson, introduction to *The Egoist*, by George Meredith (Boston: Houghton Mifflin, 1958), viii.
4. Ibid.
5. *Messalina of the Suburbs* (London, 1923) dedicated to "M. P. P." (Dr. Margaret Posthuma).
6. Delafield to Marjorie Watts, 15 September 1919.

*Chapter Three*

1. Robert Graves and Alan Hodge, *The Long Week-End: A Social History of Great Britain 1918–1939* (New York: W. W. Norton & Co., 1963), chap. 16.
2. *The Chip and the Block* (London, 1925), 252; hereafter cited in the text as *CB.*
3. *Jill* (London, 1926), 186.
4. *The Way Things Are* (London, 1927), 25; hereafter cited in the text as *W.*

*Chapter Four*

1. *Time and Tide,* 19 January 1923.
2. Margaret Rhondda, "E. M. Delafield," ibid., 13 December 1947.
3. Ibid., 22 October 1926.
4. Ibid., 19 October 1928.
5. Ibid., 8 April 1933.
6. "The Armenian Express," ibid., 25 March 1933.
7. Ibid., 4 November 1933.
8. Ibid., 7 August 1935.
9. Ibid., 8 November 1935.
10. "When Bloomsbury Meets," *Punch,* 22 May 1935.
11. Ibid., 21 April 1937.

*Chapter Five*

1. "The Diary of the Provincial Lady," in *Titles to Fame,* ed. D. K. Roberts (London, 1937), 123. All quotations relating to the

*Diary's* genesis are drawn from this chapter.

2. "Russia," *Punch*, 10 February 1937.

3. *New York Times*, "Book Review," 21 February 1937.

4. *The Provincial Lady Goes Further* (London, 1932), 72; hereafter cited in the text as *PL*.

5. *Diary of a Provincial Lady* (London, 1930), 319; hereafter cited in the text as *D*.

6. *Saturday Review of Literature*, 14 January 1933.

7. *Scots Observer*, clipping in Delafield Collection, 3–9.

8. Untitled clipping, in Delafield Collection.

9. E. M. Forester, *Aspects of the Novel* (New York: Harcourt, Brace and Company, 1927), 43.

10. W. J. Harvey, *Character and the Novel* (Ithaca: Cornell University Press, 1965), 188.

11. For example, Delafield's daughter Rosamund's *The Provincial Daughter* (New York, 1961). A successful film was based upon the diaries, which also suggested the BBC's *Mrs. Dale's Diary*, a successful series of ten year's duration.

12. Roberts, ed., *Titles to Fame*, 129.

*Chapter Six*

1. Delafield Collection, 1–5.

2. Ibid., 1–6.

3. *Nothing is Safe* (London, 1937), 167; hereafter cited in the text as *N*.

4. *Late and Soon* (London, 1943), 88; hereafter cited in the text as *L*.

5. *Thank Heaven Fasting* (London, 1932), 15, 98, 63; hereafter cited in the text as *TH*.

6. John A. Lester, Jr., "Thackeray's Narrative Technique," in *Victorian Literature*, ed. Robert O. Preyer (New York, Harper and Row, 1966), 159–81. Preyer finds that between author-narration and the finished scene, Thackeray used a variety of small, unlocated semi-scenes. Delafield uses such scenes also.

7. Delafield Collection, 1–6.

*Chapter Seven*

1. "The Angevins, The Plantagenets, and Ourselves," *Punch*, 6 September, 13 September, and 20 September 1939.

2. *Punch*, 27 September, 1 November, 29 November, and 6 December 1939.

3. "Effect of Reading the Papers," *Punch*, 5 November 1939.

4. *Punch,* 27 January 1941.

5. Ibid., 5 June 1940.

6. Ibid., 27 March 1940.

7. *Dundee Telegraph,* clipping in Delafield Collection, 3–8.

8. Delafield to Hamish Hamilton, 26 November 1940.

9. *Punch,* 10 September 1941.

10. *Time and Tide,* 7 March 1941; "Letters to the Editor," ibid., 21 March 1941.

11. Ibid., 26 July 1941.

12. *Punch,* 11 November 1942.

13. "Explanation For My Aunt," *Punch,* 21 April 1943.

14. *Punch,* 27 October 1943.

15. Ibid., 27 January 1943.

16. Richard Price, *A History of Punch* (London: Collins, 1963), 270.

17. *No One Now Will Know* (London, 1942), 278; hereafter cited in the text as *NO.*

18. Robert Rodgers, *The Double in Literature* (Detroit: Wayne State University Press, 1970), 63–64.

19. Ibid., 110.

20. Delafield to Hamish Hamilton, 26 November 1940.

21. I am indebted to Terence Pepper of the National Portrait Gallery, London, for permission to view Coster's photographs of Elizabeth and Kate.

*Chapter Eight*

1. *St. Martin's Review,* June 1940. Delafield wrote several articles on C. M. Yonge in 1940 for this review and the *Oxford Magazine.* In the September *Oxford* she avers that Yonge's immense output presents "a picture . . . of the real, everyday life of the period" and explains her attraction during wartime. First, Yonge provides for a nostalgic escape into the safe past. Second, her novels "breathe on every page a most fervent and unquestioning belief in the ultimate power of right over wrong, and the worthwhileness of plain, simple goodness."

2. *The Bazalgettes* (London, 1935), 340; hereafter cited in the text as *B.*

3. "To See Ourselves," act 2, sc. 2.

4. *The British Character by Pont,* intro. E. M. Delafield (London: Collins, 1938). She liked this line so well that she repeated it a year later in "To See Ourselves."

5. *Man, Proud Man,* ed. Mabel Ulrich (London, 1932), 70.

6. Moers, *Literary Women,* iv.

7. J. B. Priestley, *English Humour* (New York, 1976), 115.

8. David Worcester, *The Art of Satire* (New York: W. W. Norton, 1969), 73, 11, 129.

9. "The Funny Side of it All," *Punch,* 24 March 1939. Despite the slight slipping of the comic mask in this complaint, the sketch closes with the I-narrator turning back to her desk to make a humorous article from bank statements, doctor's bills, and the like.

10. David Daiches, *The Present Age* (Bloomington, 1950), 282. Typically, following Daiches's note an incomplete list of Delafield's works is appended.

11. Henry Bergson, "Laughter," in *Comedy,* ed. Wylie Sypher (Baltimore: Johns Hopkins University Press, 1980).

12. Ibid., 127.

13. *The Provincial Lady in Wartime* (London, 1939), 46; hereafter cited in the text as *PW.*

14. *Punch,* 10 September 1935.

15. Bergson, "Laughter," 67.

16. Samuel Chew, *A Literary History of England,* ed. Albert C. Baugh (New York: Appleton-Century-Crofts, 1948), 1203–4; *Jane Austen: Twentieth Century Interpretations of Pride and Prejudice,* ed. E. Rubinstein (Englewood Cliffs, N. J.: Prentice-Hall, 1963), 9, 1, 5.

17. Malcolm Bradbury, *Possibilities: Essays on the State of the Novel* (London: Oxford University Press, 1973), 47.

# Selected Bibliography

PRIMARY SOURCES

1. Novels

*Zella Sees Herself.* London: Heinemann, 1917.

*The War Workers.* London: Heinemann, 1918.

*The Pelicans.* London: Heinemann, 1918.

*Consequences.* London: Hodder and Stoughton, 1919.

*Tension.* London: Hutchinson, 1920.

*The Heel of Achilles.* London: Hutchinson, 1920.

*Humbug.* London: Hutchinson, 1921.

*The Optimist.* London: Hutchinson, 1922.

*A Reversion to Type.* London: Hutchinson, 1923.

*Messalina of the Suburbs.* London: Hutchinson, 1923.

*Mrs. Harter.* London: Hutchinson, 1924.

*The Chip and the Block.* London: Hutchinson, 1925.

*Jill.* London: Hutchinson, 1926.

*The Way Things Are.* London: Hutchinson, 1927.

*What is Love* (U. S. title: *First Love*). London: Macmillan, 1928. Macmillan had previously published Delafield's novels in the United States. When this company became Delafield's publisher in England, Harper's became her U. S. publisher. Her major continental publisher was Tauchniz, who published at least nine titles.

*The Suburban Young Man.* London: Macmillan, 1928.

*Diary of a Provincial Lady.* London: Macmillan, 1930.

*Turn Back the Leaves.* London: Macmillan, 1930.

*Challenge to Clarissa* (U. S. title: *House Party*). London: Macmillan, 1931.

*Thank Heaven Fasting* (U. S. title: *A Good Man's Love*). London: Macmillan, 1932.

*The Provincial Lady Goes Further* (U. S. title: *The Provincial Lady in London*). London: Macmillan, 1932.

*Gay Life.* London: Macmillan, 1933.

*The Provincial Lady in America.* London: Macmillan, 1934.

*The Bazalgettes.* London: Hamish Hamilton, 1935.

*Faster! Faster!* London: Macmillan, 1936.

*Nothing Is Safe.* London: Macmillan, 1937.
*The Provincial Lady in Wartime.* London: Macmillan, 1939.
*No One Now Will Know.* London: Macmillan, 1942.
*Late and Soon.* London: Macmillan, 1943.

2. Other Fiction
*The Entertainment.* London: Macmillan, 1926. Short stories.
*Women Are Like That.* London: Macmillan, 1929. Short stories.
*Three Marriages* (U. S. title: *When Women Love*) London: Macmillan, 1939. Novella.
*Love Has No Resurrection.* London: Macmillan, 1941. Short stories.

3. Plays
*To See Ourselves.* London: French, 1931. Reprinted in *Famous Plays of 1931* (London, Gollancz, 1931).
*The Glass Wall.* London, Gollancz, 1933.
"The Mulberry Bush." BBC Radio broadcast, 19 July 1935. Unpublished.

4. Other Work: Contributions, Introductions, Miscellanies
*Man, Proud Man.* Edited by Mabel Ulrich. London: Hamish Hamilton, 1932.
*Time and Tide Album.* Edited by E. M. Delafield. London: Hamish Hamilton, 1932.
*General Impressions.* London: Macmillan, 1933.
*The Brontes.* Compiled, with introduction, by E. M. Delafield. London: Hogarth, 1935.
*Straw Without Bricks* (U. S. title: *I Visit the Soviets*). London: Macmillan, 1937.
*As Others Hear Us.* London: Macmillan, 1937.
*Ladies and Gentlemen in Victorian Fiction.* London: Hogarth, 1937.
*Charlotte Mary Yonge.* By Georgina Battiscombe. Introduction by E. M. Delafield. London: Constable, 1943.
*People You Love.* London: Collins, 1940.


SECONDARY SOURCES


Canby, Henry Seidel. "Charm with Irony." *Saturday Review of Literature,* 14 January 1933, 376. Review of *The Provincial Lady in London* (U. S. title: *The Provincial Lady Goes Further*). This most perceptive review recognizes her as a distinguished novelist of manners.

**Daiches, David.** *The Present Age.* Bloomington: Indiana University Press, 1950. A small note, but the only one by a respected literary historian—to which an incomplete list of Delafield's work is appended!

**Price, Richard.** *A History of Punch.* London: Collins, 1963. Price recognizes Delafield's contribution, but restricts her subject matter to the country gentry.

**Priestley, Joseph.** *English Humour.* New York: Stein & Day, 1976. Brief, descriptive, and restricted to her humor, this is still the most important recognition of her talent since her death.

**Rhondda, Vicountess Margaret.** "E. M. Delafield." *Time and Tide,* 13 December 1947. A sensitive obituary notice praising Delafield's journalism.

**Roberts, D. K.** *Titles to Fame.* London: Nelson, 1937. A lightly edited anecdotal discussion of the genesis of and response to the Provincial Lady books mostly written by Delafield herself. It excludes the later *Provincial Lady in Wartime.* Noteworthy for authoritative background and Delafield's characteristic disclaimers that her diaries have any literary merit.

This study is the first serious criticism of Delafield's work. Some explanation of this unfortunate if understandable situation appears above, especially in the preface and the conclusion to chapter 5. Additionally, when after World War II several Delafield projects were begun, family recalcitrance, the death of her close friends, the difficulties in dealing with her large, mixed production, and the unavailability of her work caused their cancellations. The acquisition of Delafield materials was an exciting but tedious quest.

Two examples. Her beautifully produced literary spoof, *The Bazalgettes,* indexed by the British Library and the Library of Congress, could be located by neither of these superb national libraries, probably because it is unsigned. Hamish Hamilton, its publisher, may possess the only available copy in the world. A play, "The Mulberry Bush," proved even harder to find. Listed in *The Present Age,* David Daiches generously but unsuccessfully tried to track down his citation. Laura Boyer, University of the Pacific reference librarian, corroborated Daiches's citation only after a search of two years and patient help from English librarians, who led her finally to the B.B.C.—and a copy of the broadcast script.

Faced with such difficulties, a scholar turns naturally to book reviews, and reviewers' critical approaches to Delafield's books may be summarized as follows:

The major agreement among reviewers early or late, American as well as English, was the immediate and persistent comparison with Jane Austen. The reviewer of *Zella* for the *Nation* (8 November 1917), noted its similarity to *Northanger Abbey* and concluded: "In its precision of characterization and dialogue as well as its well-nigh unerring satirical touch, it measurably suggests the great mistress of British fiction." As Delafield was a new talent and the daughter of a famous novelist, the first English reviewers tended to enlarge on the comparison. In the *London World Today* (February 1918), Delafield was praised for "a power of keen observation, a delicate satirical sense, and that rarest of all qualities, humour. She can outline a character in a few brief strokes, and produce a perfect little vignette such as one must go to the works of Jane Austen to equal."

Delafield's realistic satiric vein received nearly universal praise. Adjectives like "honest," "precise," and "acute" pick up her shrewd, insightful powers of observation. Another set of repeated terms show reviewers responding to the range of her irony: "light," "dry," "dry wit" shade into "astringent" (an adjective L. P. Hartley reused), "malicious," "barbed," and "ruthless."

Recognizing the range and acuteness of her wit, reviewers also praised her best work for its sociocultural value. "An honest and challenging contribution to the sociology of the day," the *New York Times* said of *Gay Life* (15 October 1933), and similar praise was voiced for *Jill, The Way Things Are,* and *Thank Heaven Fasting.*

Praise for her characterization, wit, and "perfect social pictures colored by irony" was sometimes tempered by male critics. Just eight days after Canby's penetrating appreciation of *The Provincial Lady Goes Further,* Louis Kronenberger added this caveat in his *New York Times* review: "The book is extraordinarily feminine, and if it lacks the breadth and color of male participation in life, is chock-full of the light awareness, the gay and undeceived alertness, that only a perceptive woman can possess." This example of the scale versus stature argument seen in male/female terms, which underlies so much criticism of women's fiction, goes back beyond Jane Austen. Certainly Delafield's adherence to domestic subjects relegated her to a minor reputation. Although reviewers seldom expanded upon it, the term "feminine" stands as a kind of shorthand notation for narrowness of vision.

A complementary criticism, lack of "depth" or "consequence," picks up the same scale versus value assumption. It is not entirely undeserved, although a thematic reassessment of Delafield's work from a feminist perspective should now perceive more depth than did some contemporary reviewers.

One further occasional criticism faulted her "sense of construction."

Delafield's predilection for deep analysis of motive, in Victorian problem novel form, did not satisfy modernists. This critical problem, addressed in the conclusion to chapter 8, is not a simple one. Here
we should note that Delafield recognized this weakness early and
worked to remedy it.

In his milestone review, Canby attempts to put "the difficulties of
belonging to the Jane Austen school in the nineteen thirties" in perspective. Observing that Delafield is somewhat too ironic, too delicate,
too concerned with everyday manners to be taken seriously "by heavy-
handed advocates of social changes," he asks: "Why has she not had
the resounding success which so many English women writers have
grown great upon?" His answer: "Because, I think, of her unpretentiousness, the unpretentiousness of one, who like Jane Austen, *seems*
[my italics] to write easily upon her lap, while others talk and clamor
around her."

As Delafield refined her technique and grew as a craftswoman, reviewers began to mention her firmer sense of structure and skillful
use of point of view. By the mid-thirties, the fact that she was under-
valued began to be pointed out. In a *Time and Tide* review on 12
November 1932, novelist Francis Iles asserted that "Miss Delafield
has always seemed to me a writer who has not received her due."
R. Ellis Roberts went further in a *Punch* review for 21 October 1933.
Arguing that novelists of less knowledge and power have higher reputations, Roberts wrote: "Yet she rarely gets the serious attention she
deserves, simply because she is so extraordinarily readable."

The pattern revealed by reviews throughout Delafield's career is
clear and accurate. As a twentieth-century descendant of the Jane Austen school, Delafield received praise when she approached the standard
of the master, but her comparable weaknesses loomed larger to post-
Jamesian critics. No Janeites have sprung to her defense, despite the
voices raised on her behalf before World War II. Although the fact
that her historical moment was not conducive to establishing a place
in literary history for her, a quarter of a century of good reviews
suggest that she deserves one.

# Index